COLOR ESCAPES

Taking control.
One affirmation at a time.

TH Warnick

Published by Coastal Escape Publishing in 2015.
First Edition, First Print

Illustrations and design @2015 TWarnick

www.colorescapes.com

ISBN: 978-0692513705

There is no right way or wrong way to express yourself with color. It's all in the eye of the beholder. As such, I've added extra pages without the words for your enjoyment should you prefer to color them instead.

Have fun.

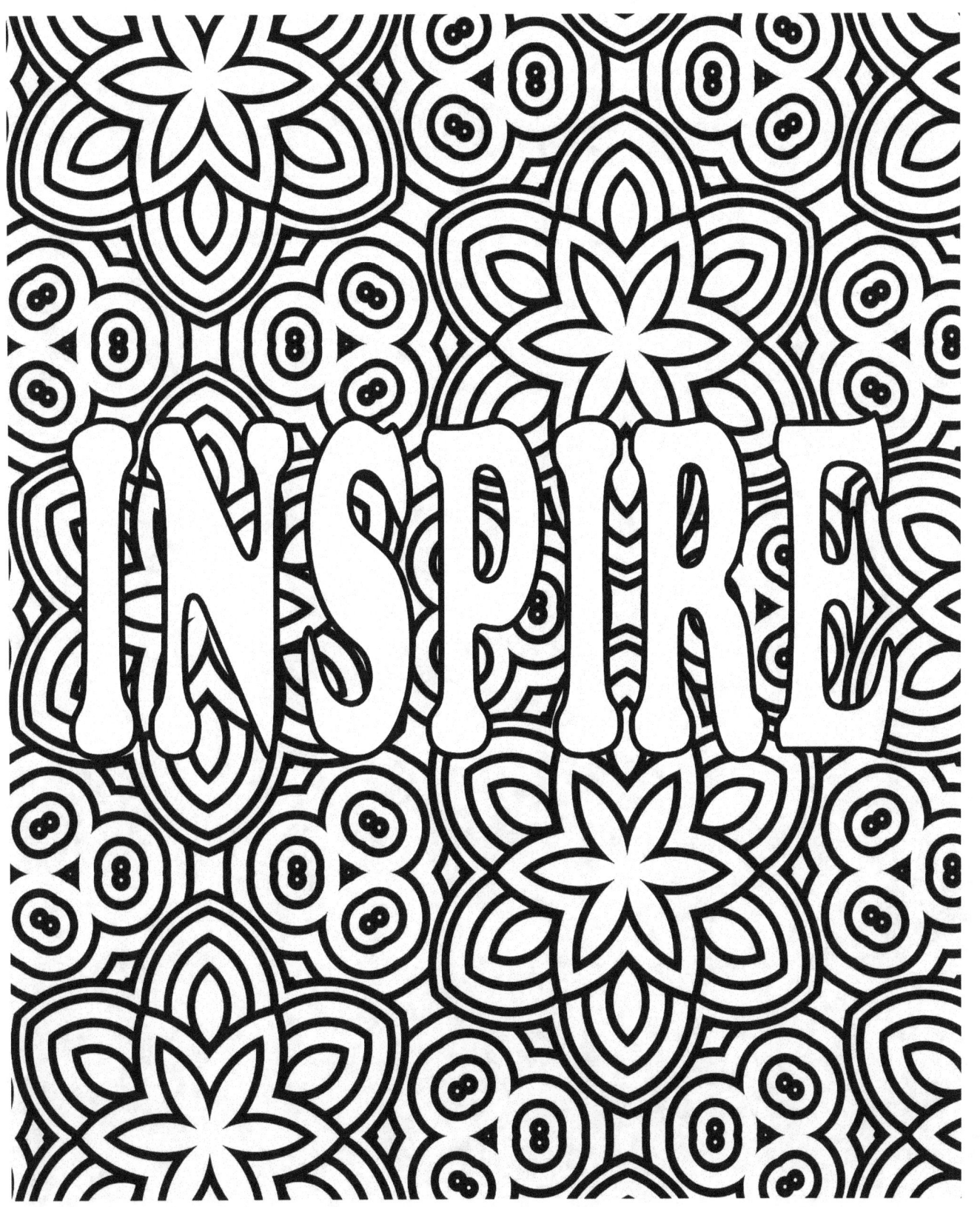

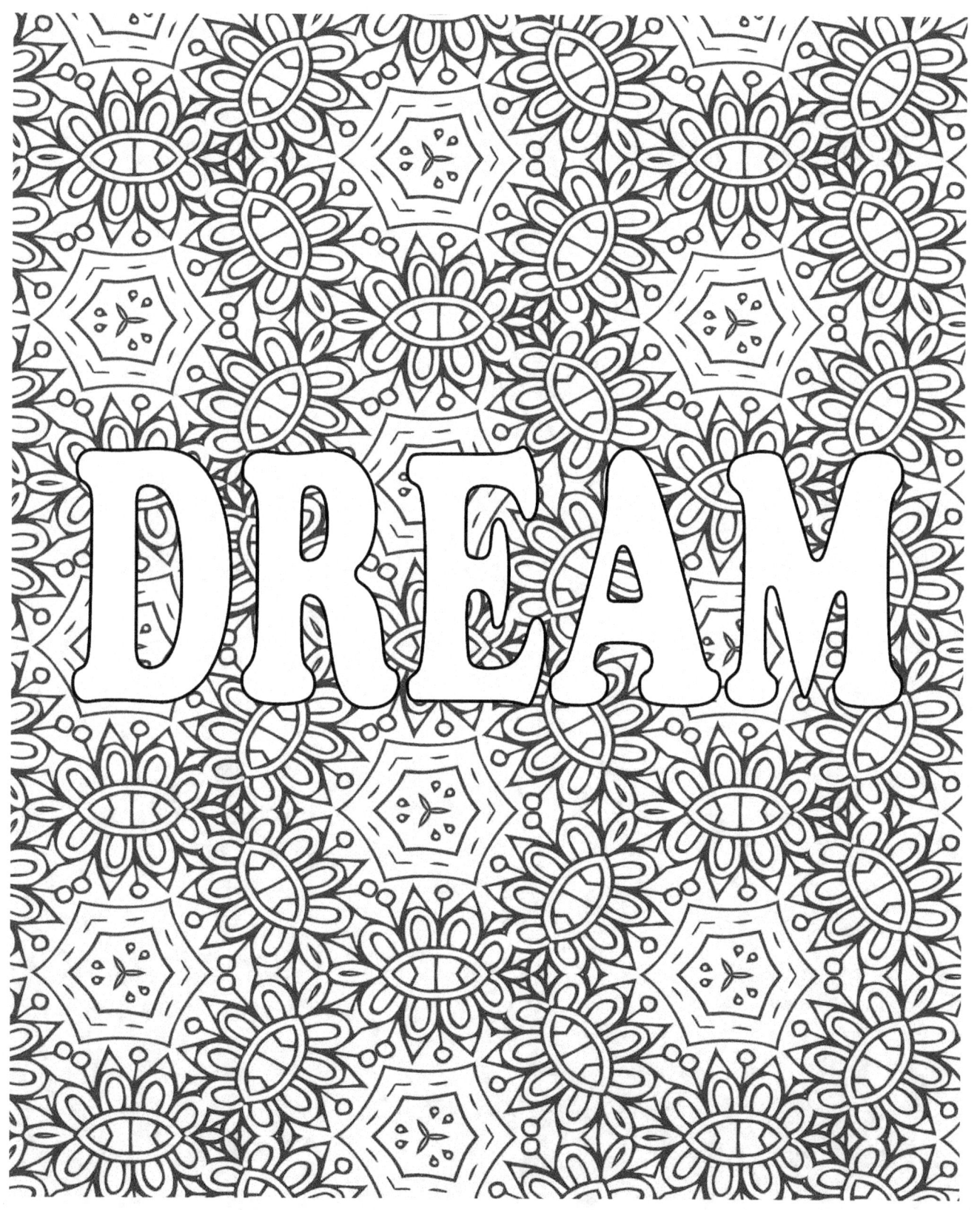

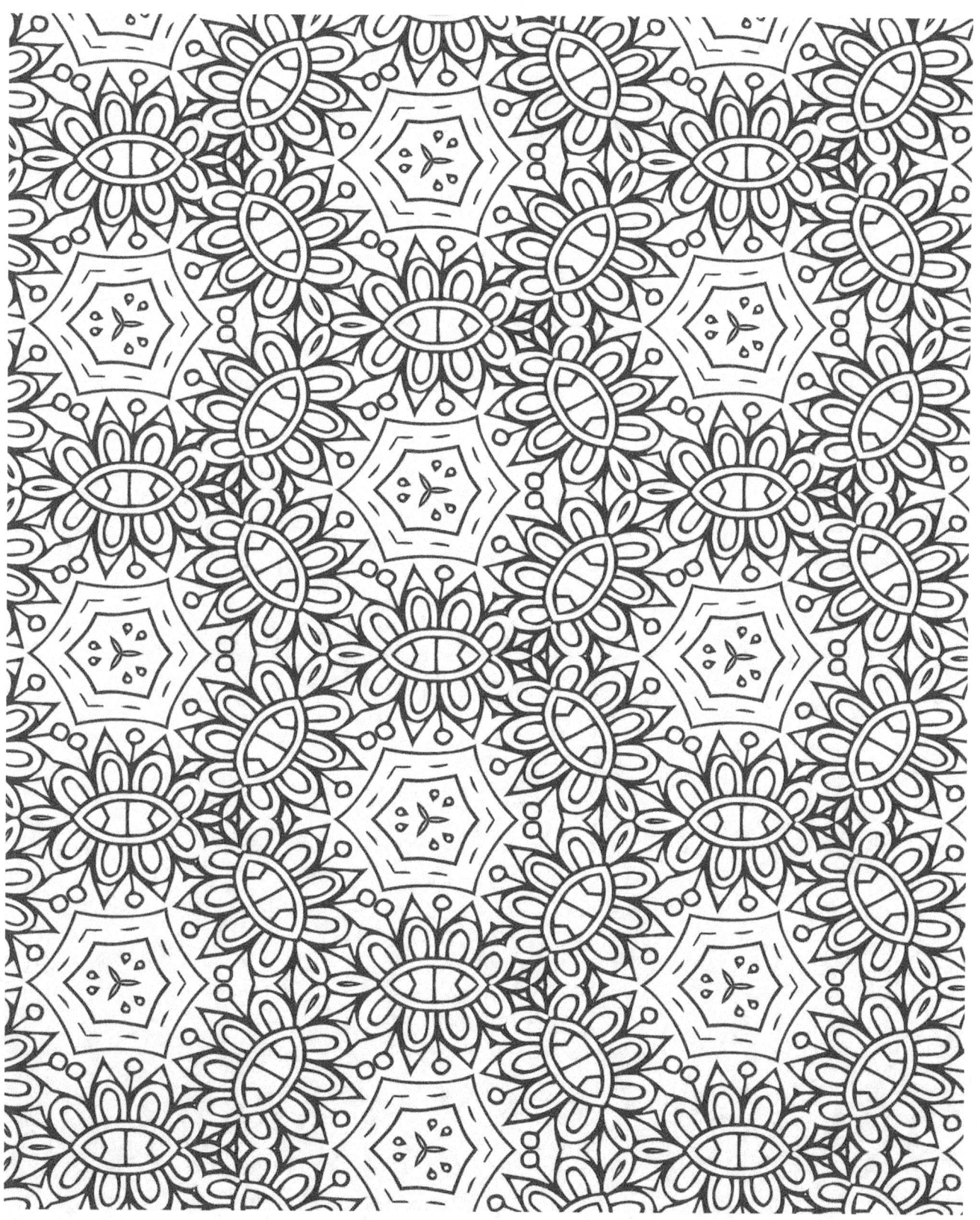

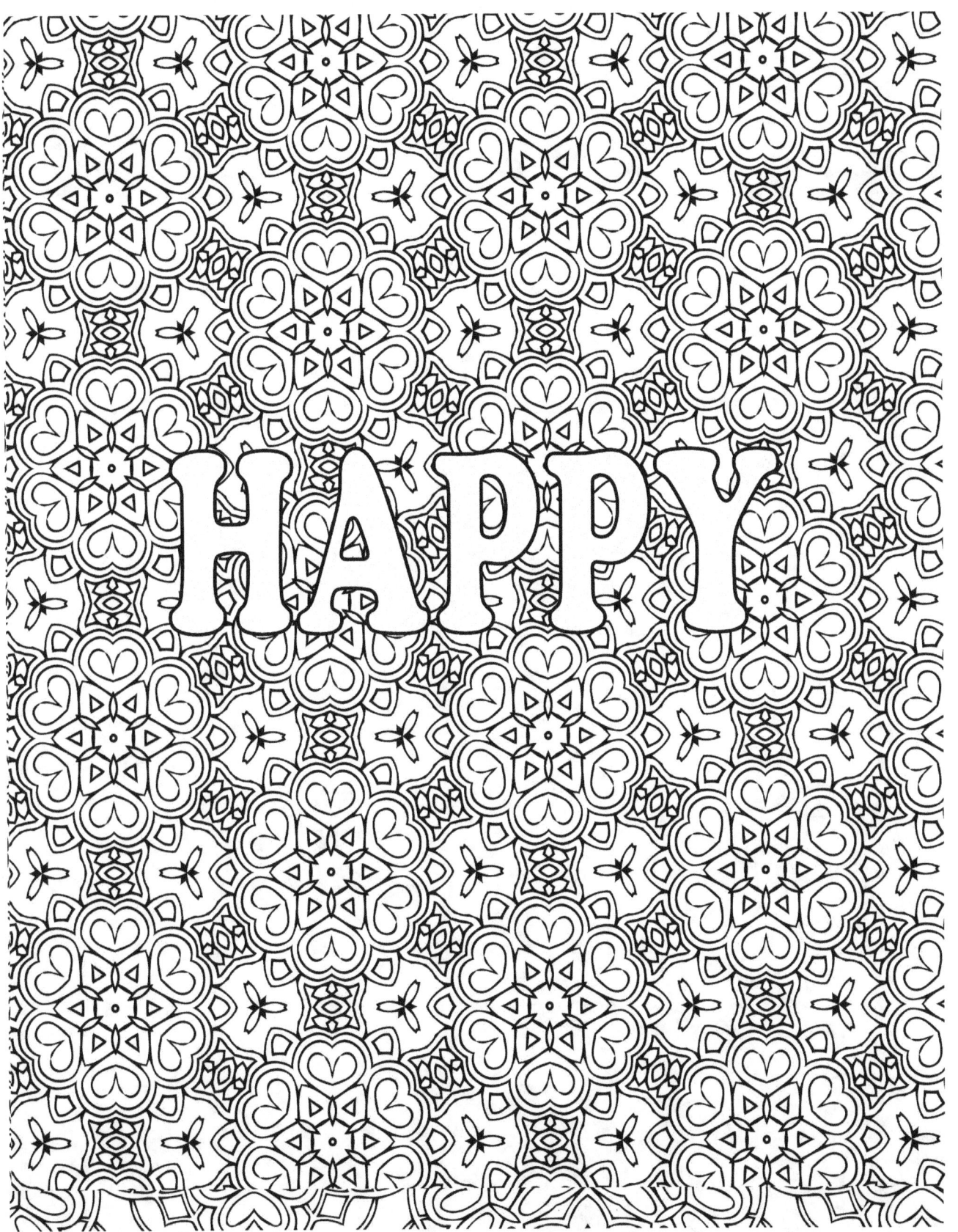

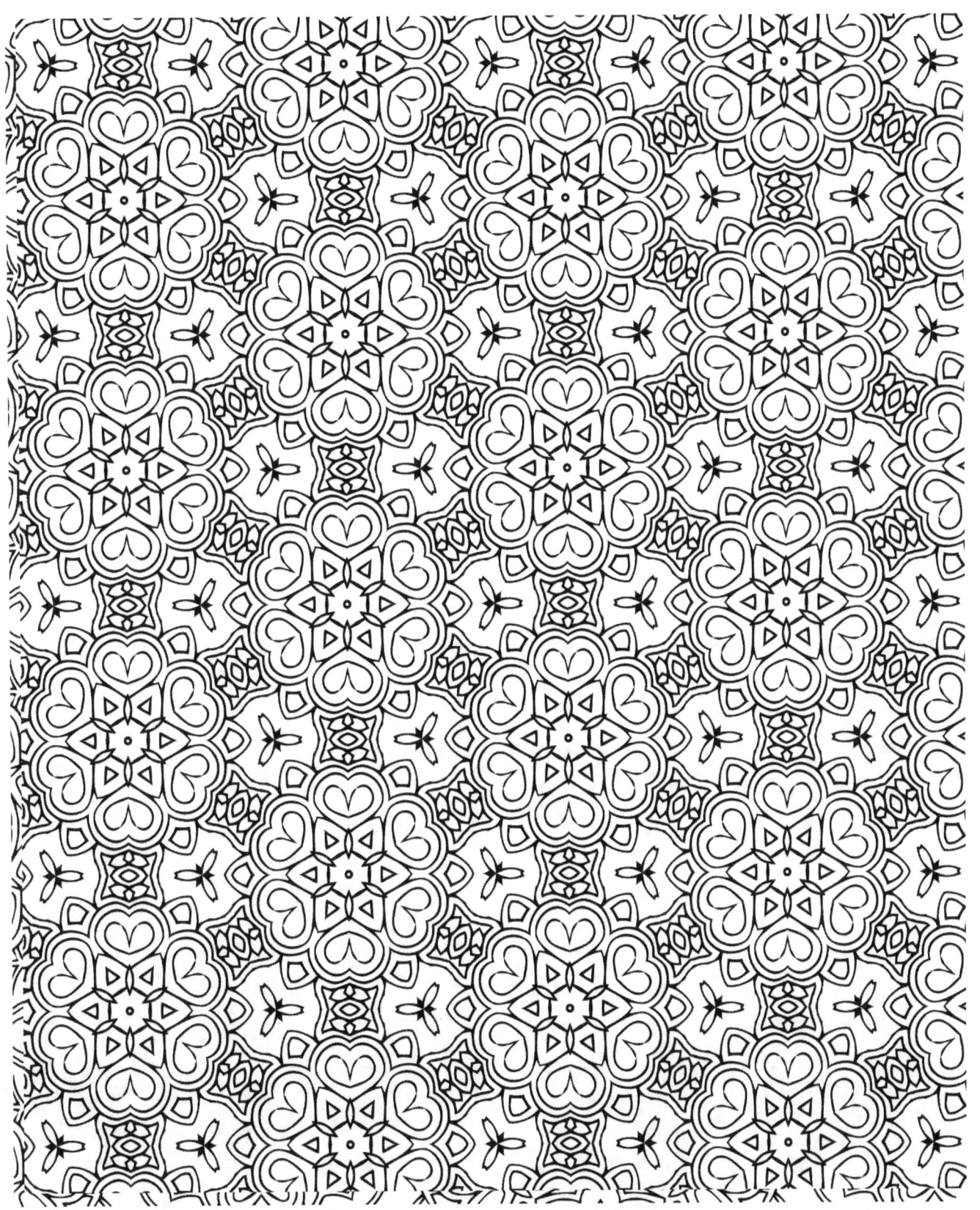

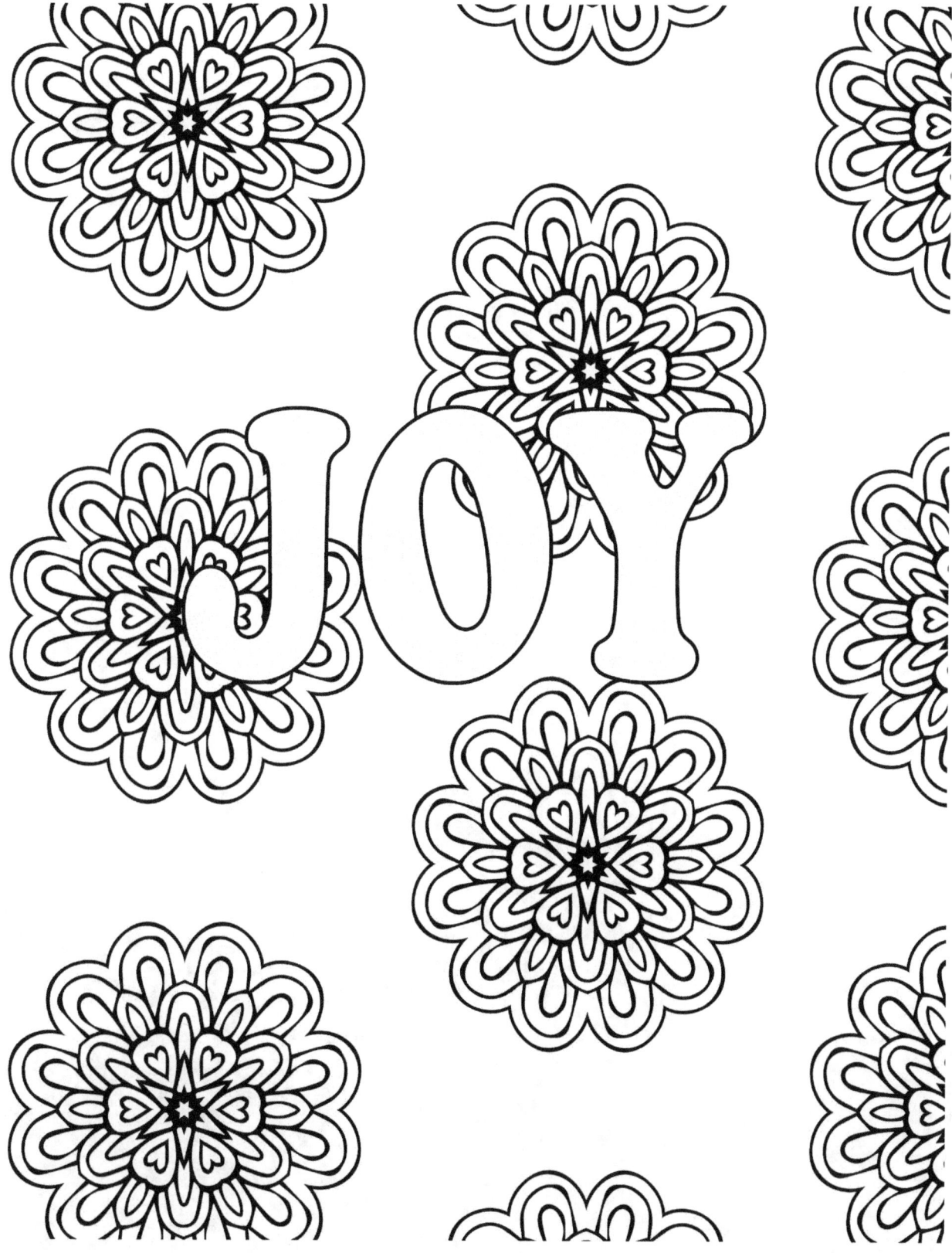

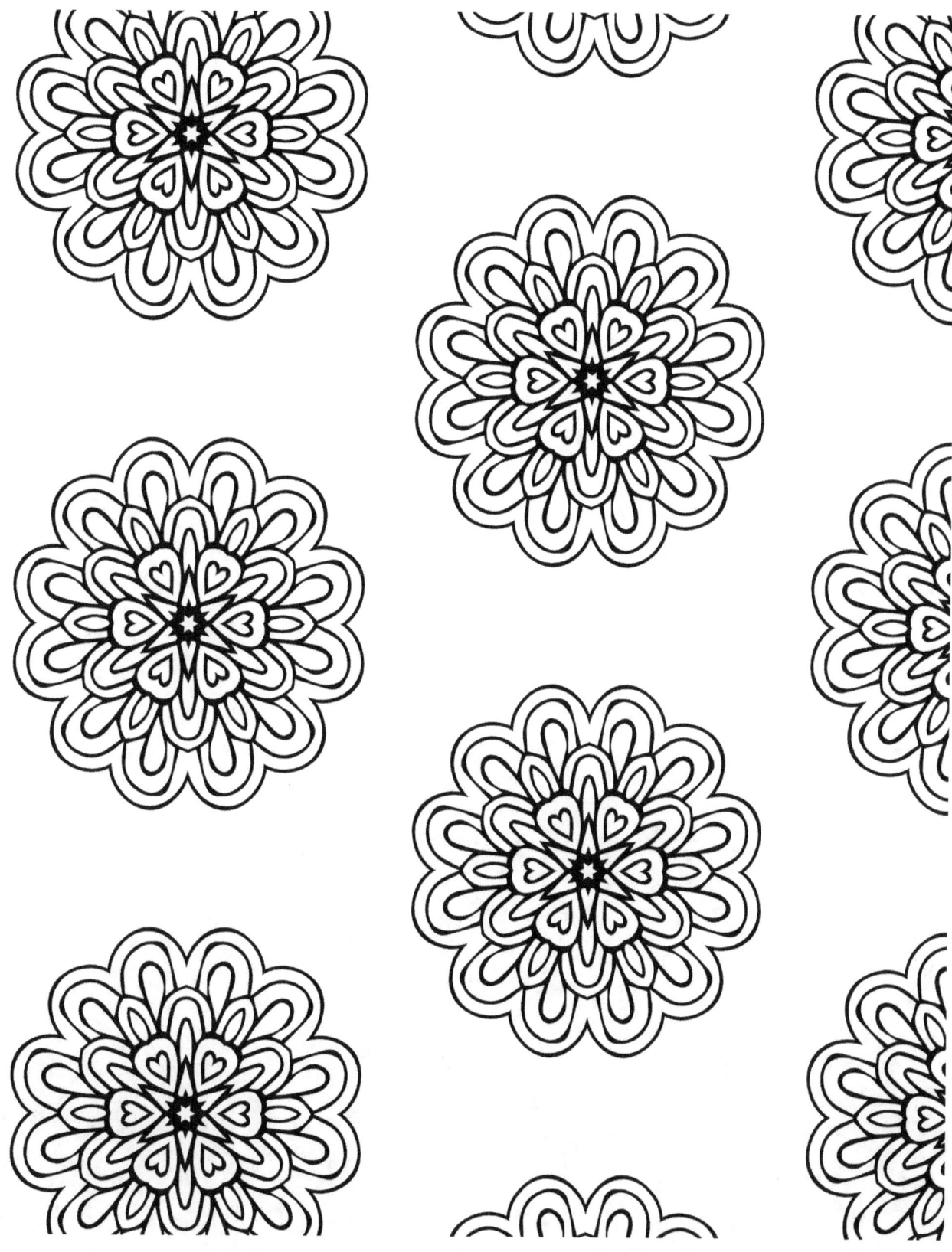

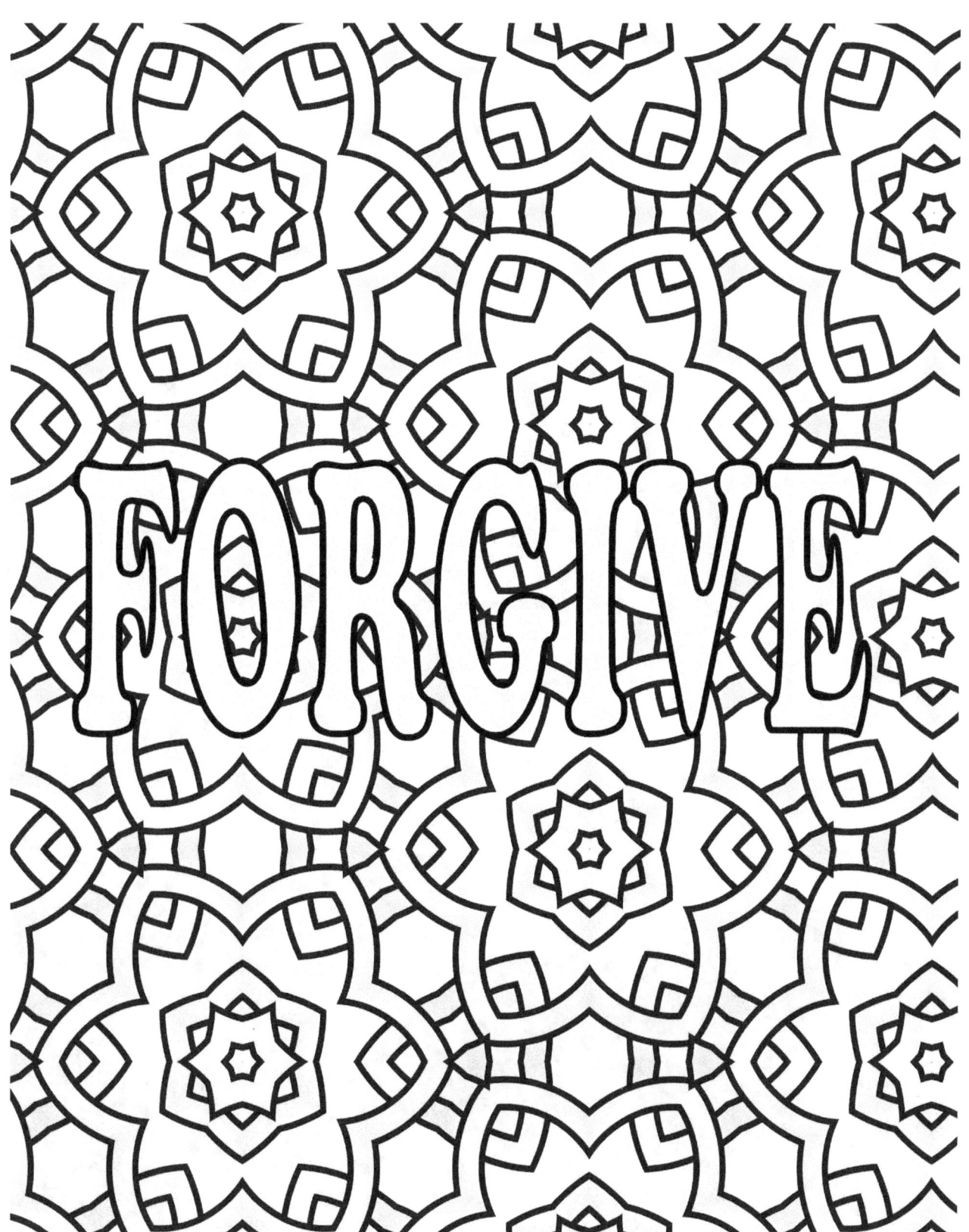

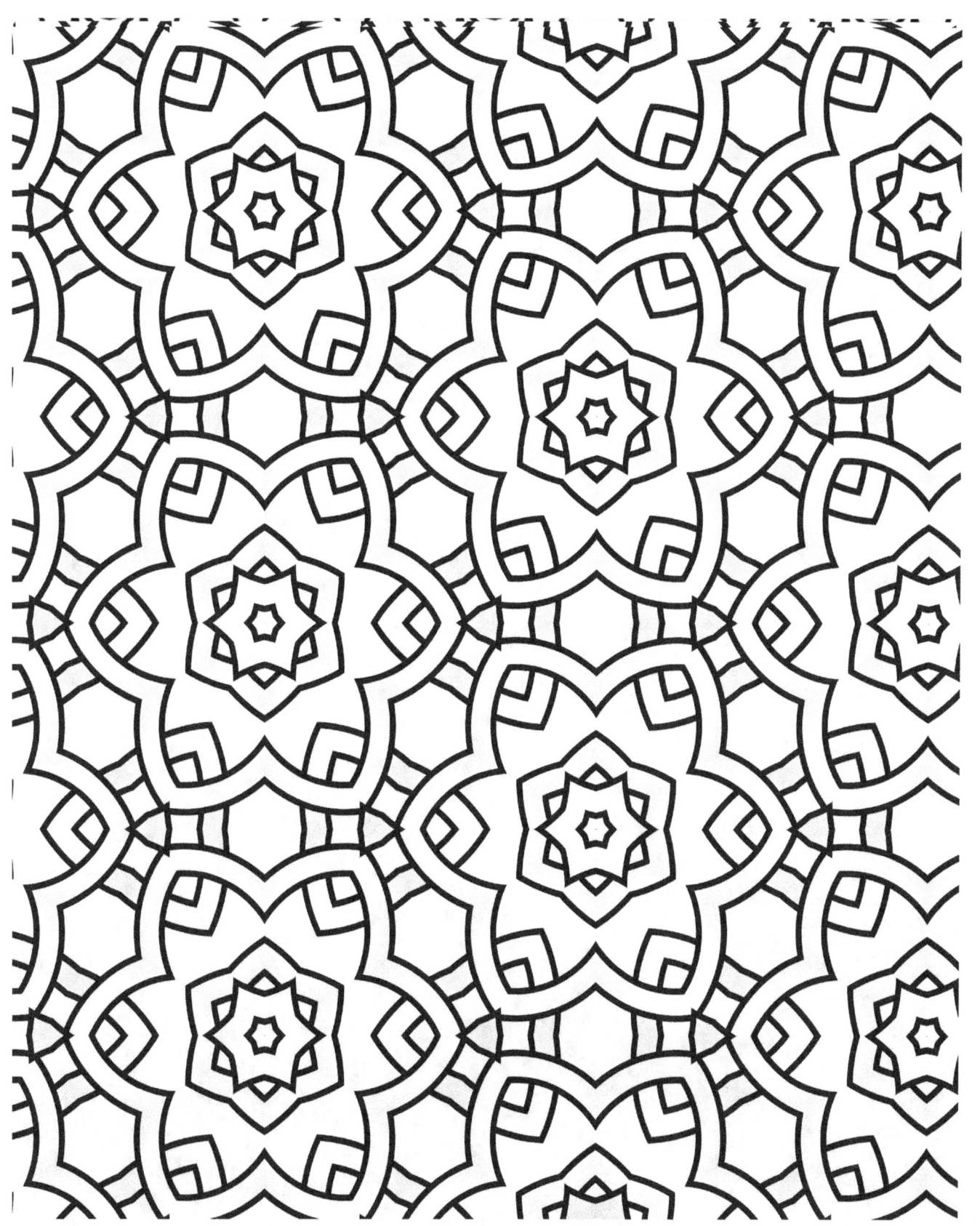

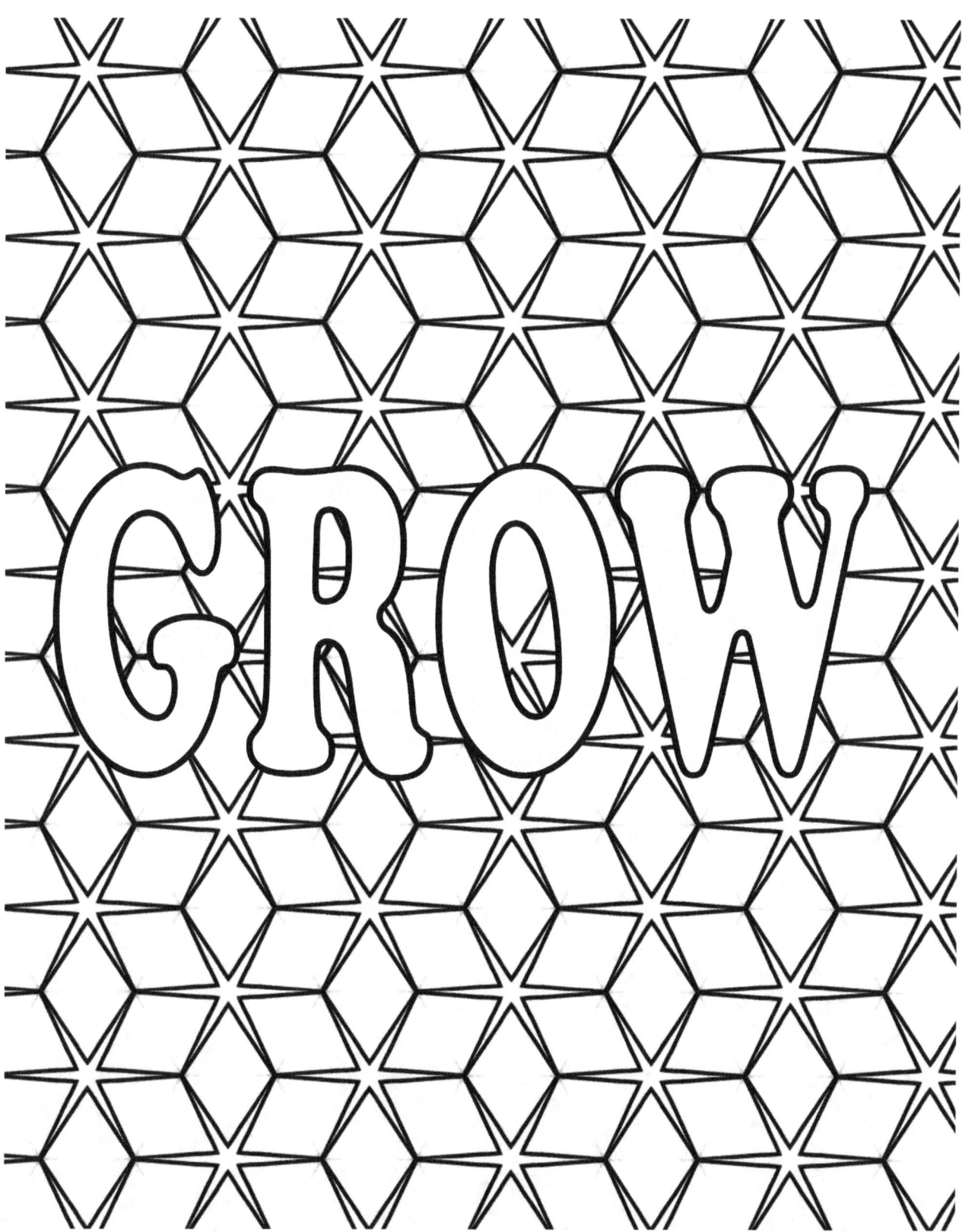

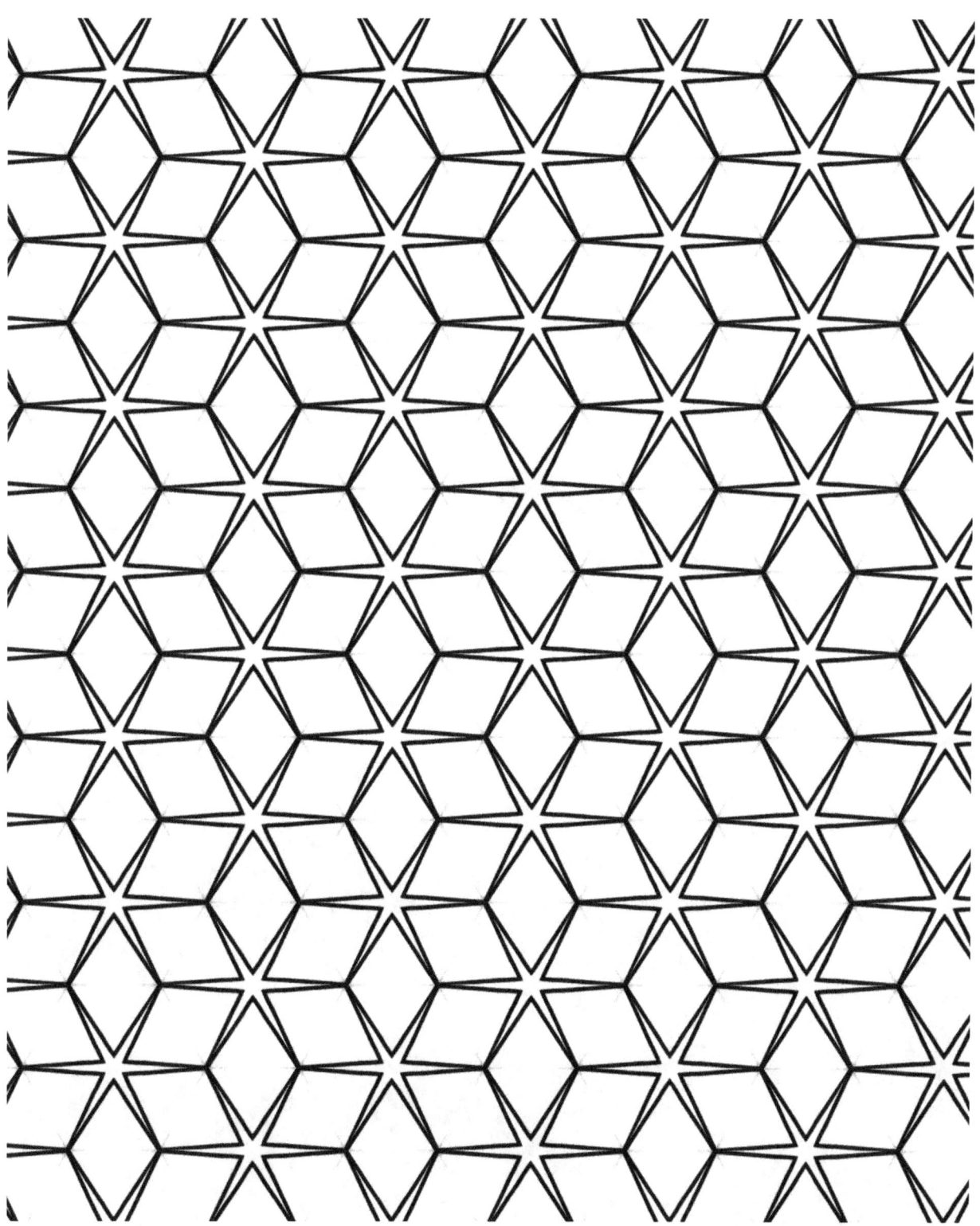

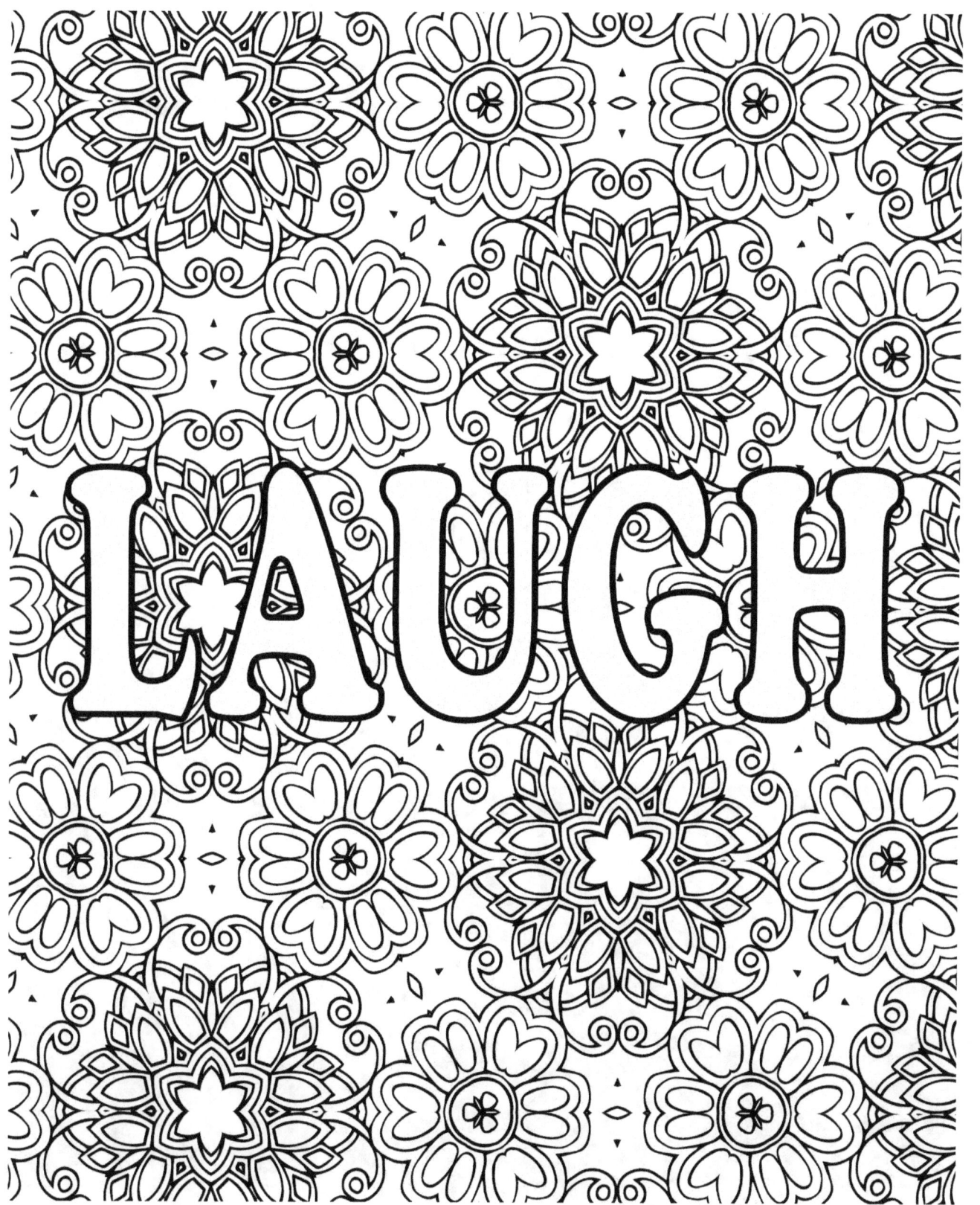

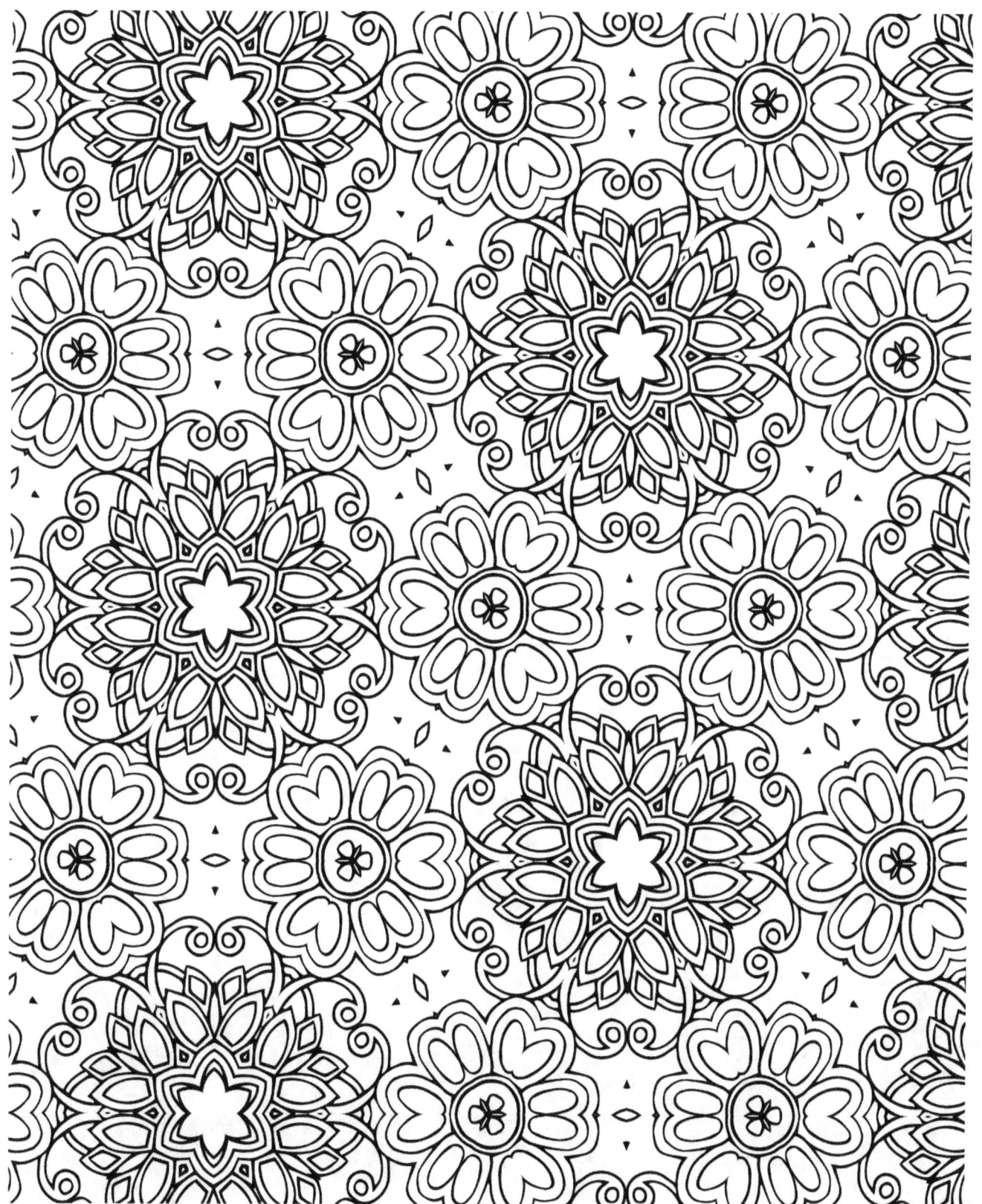

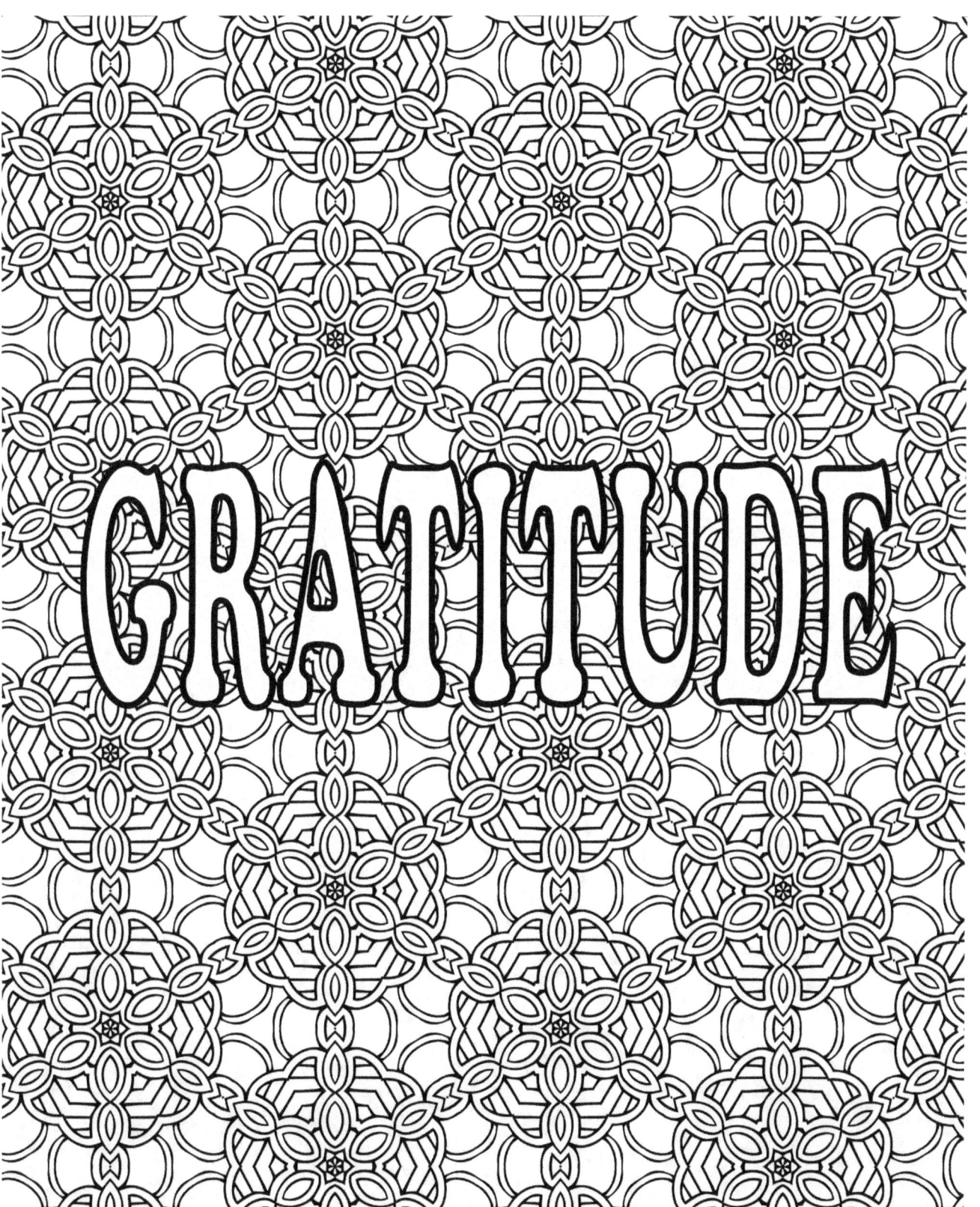

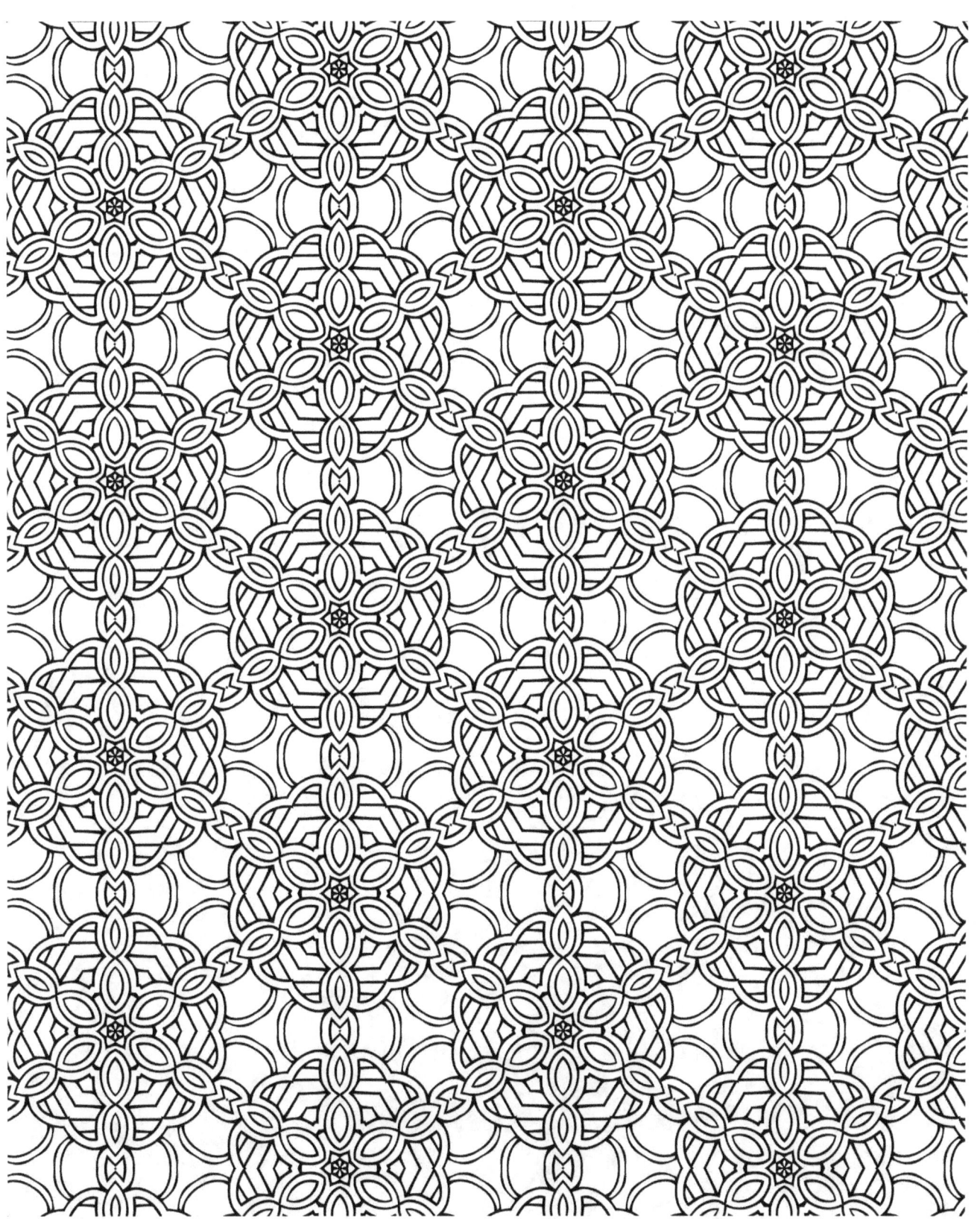

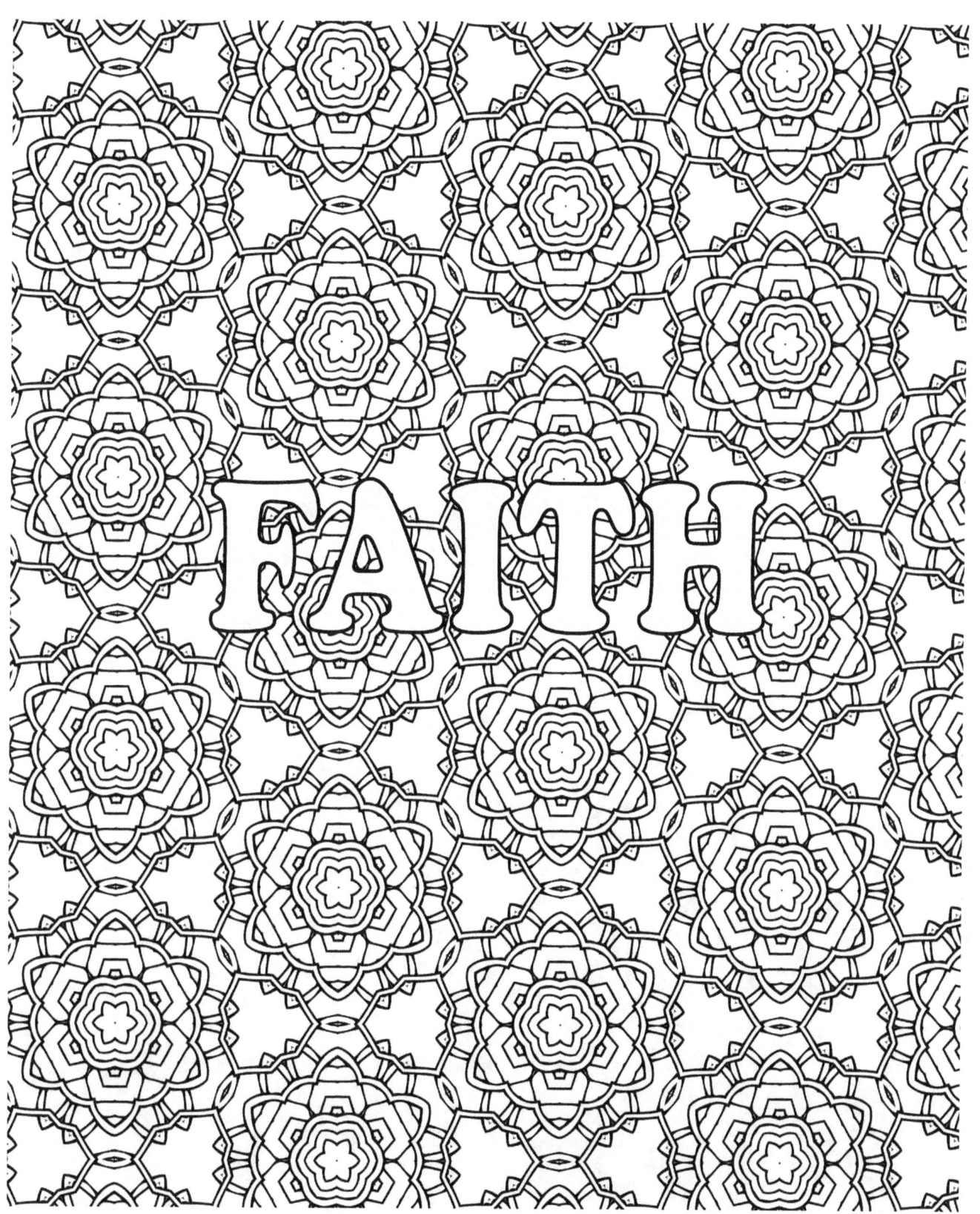

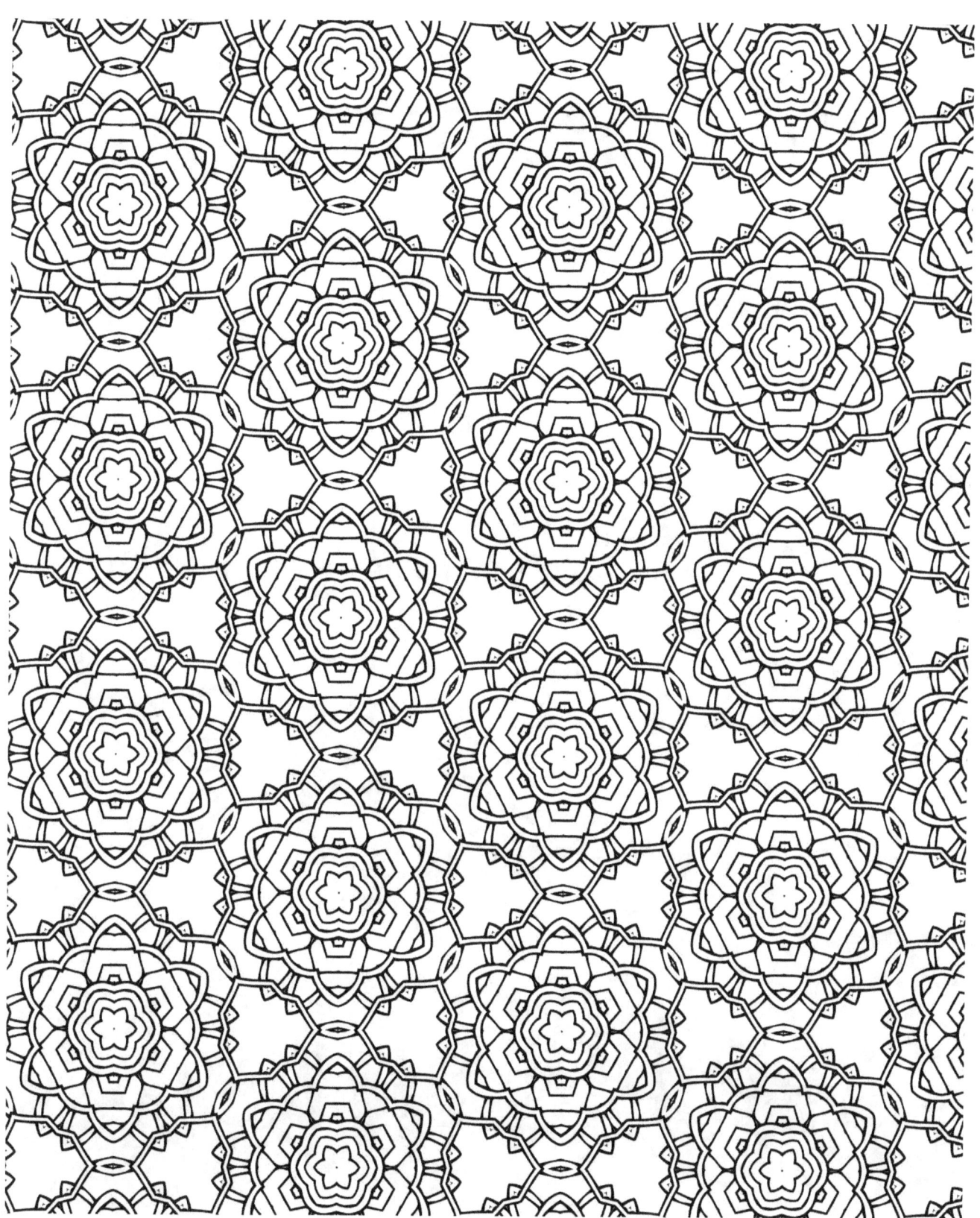

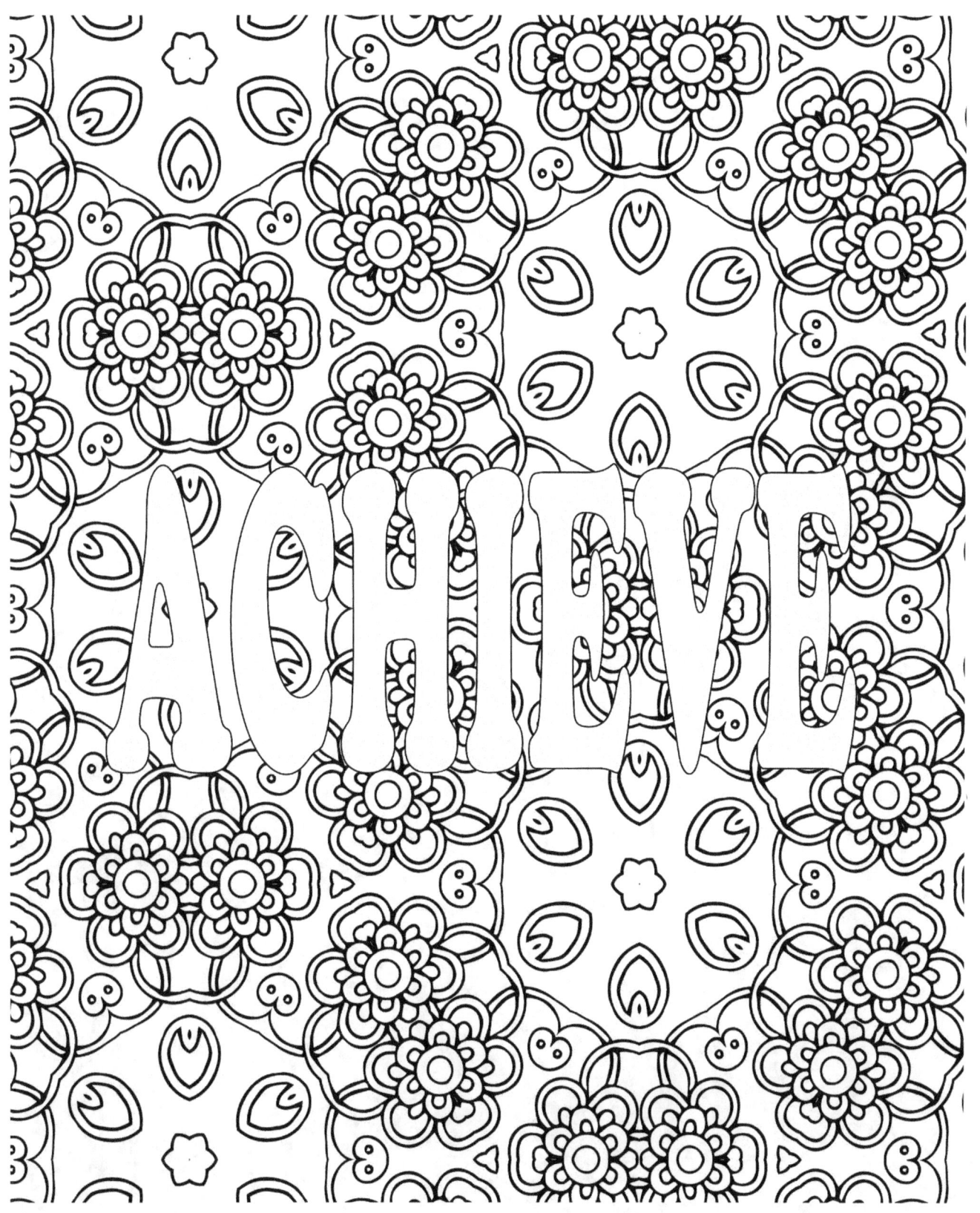

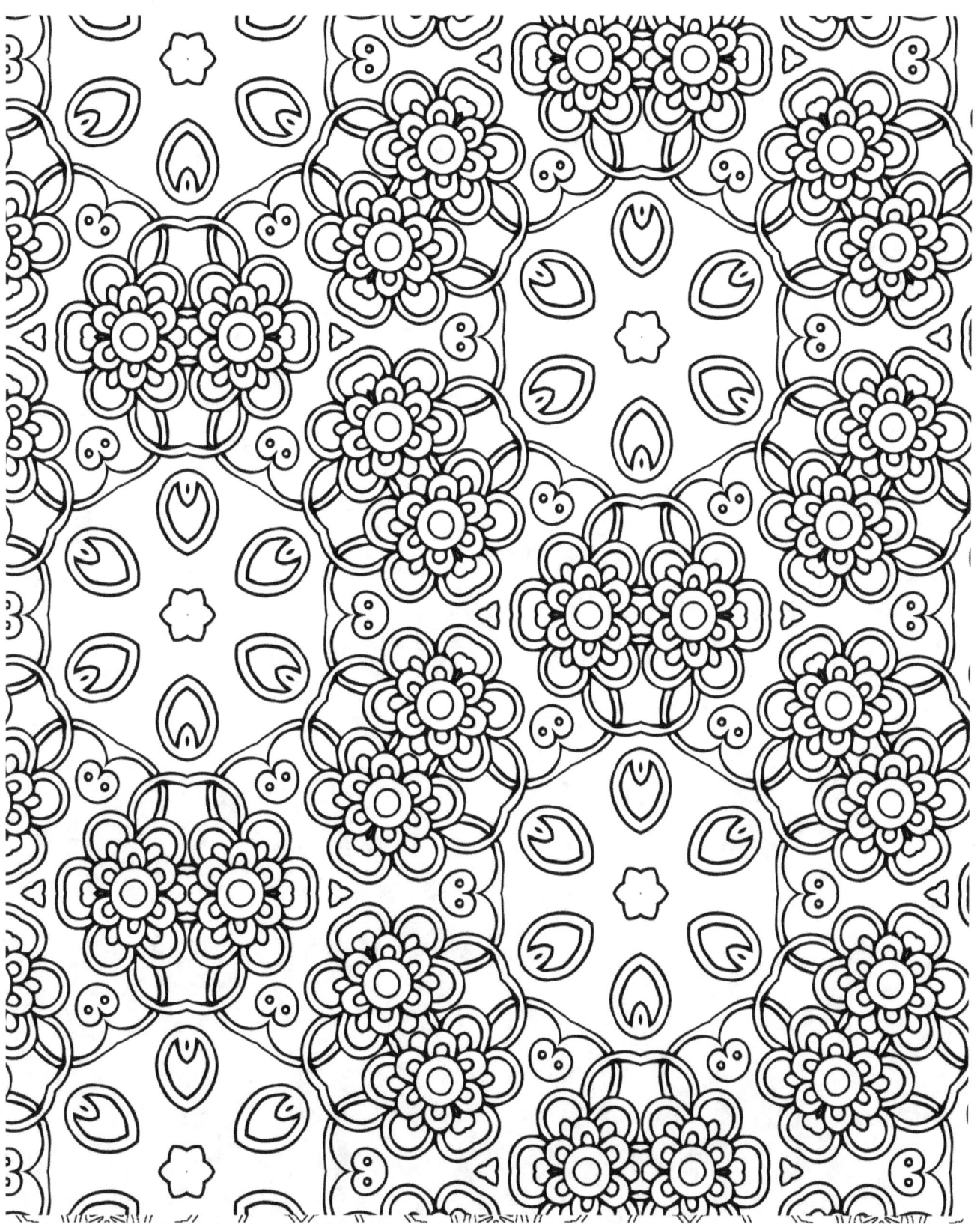

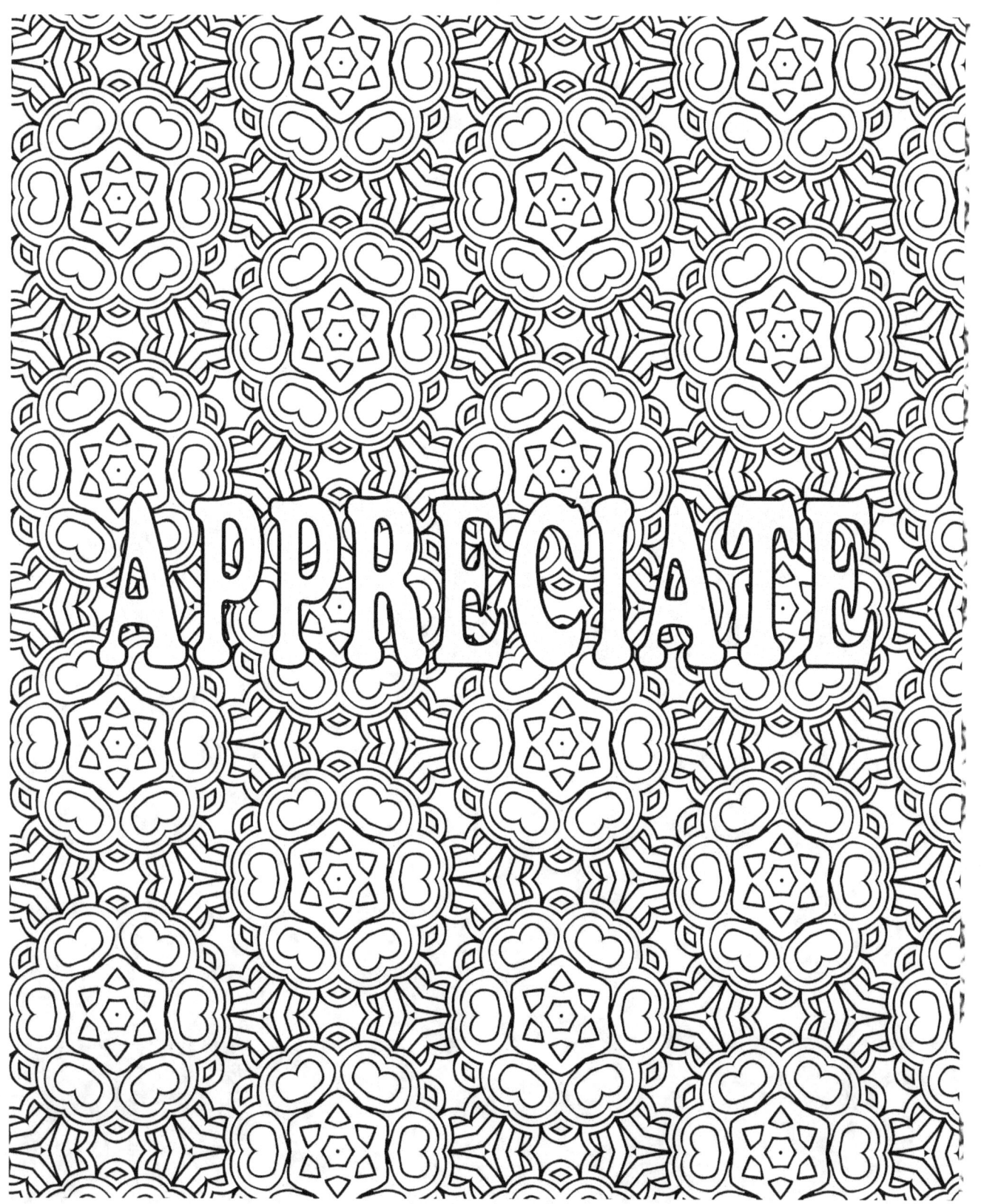

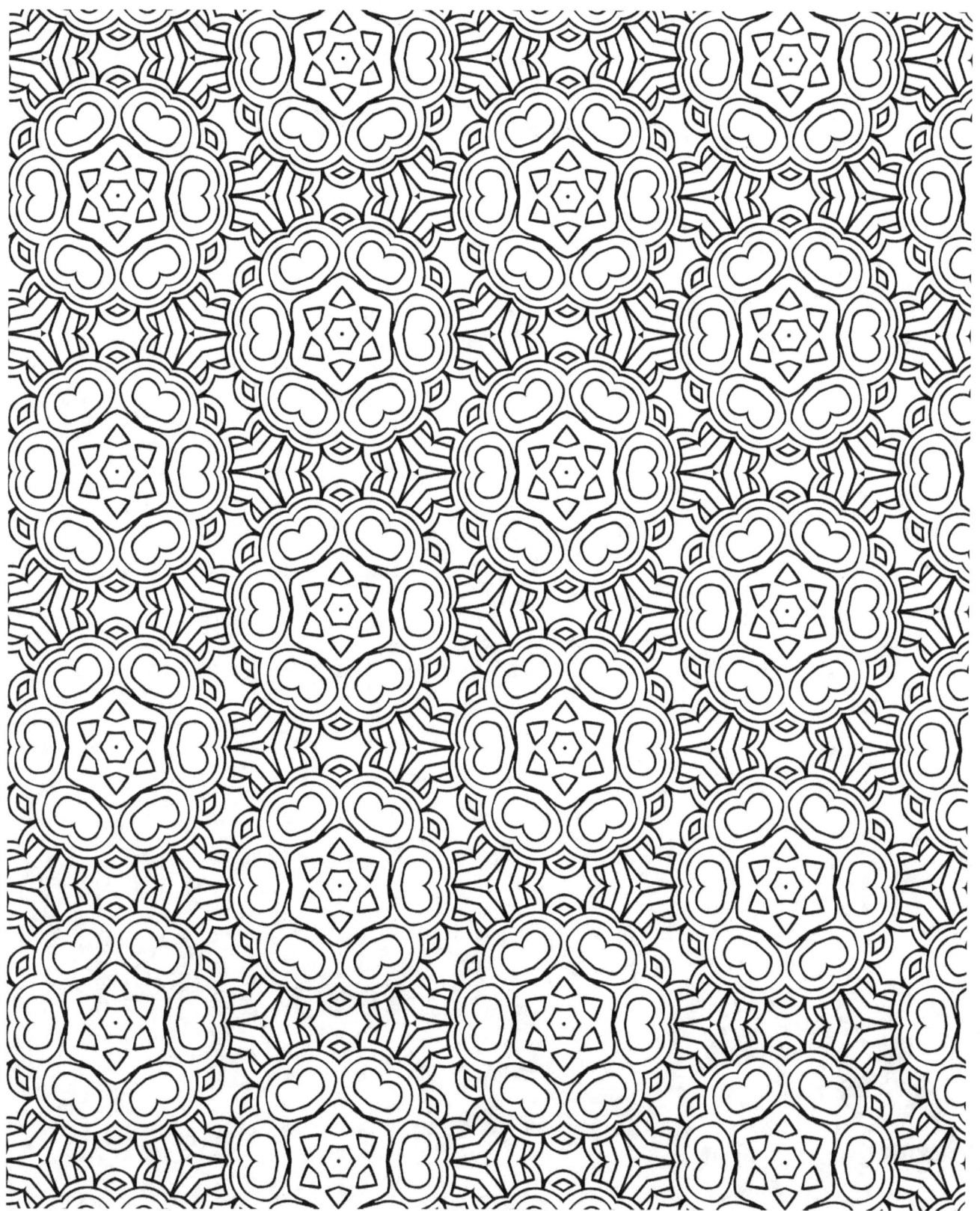

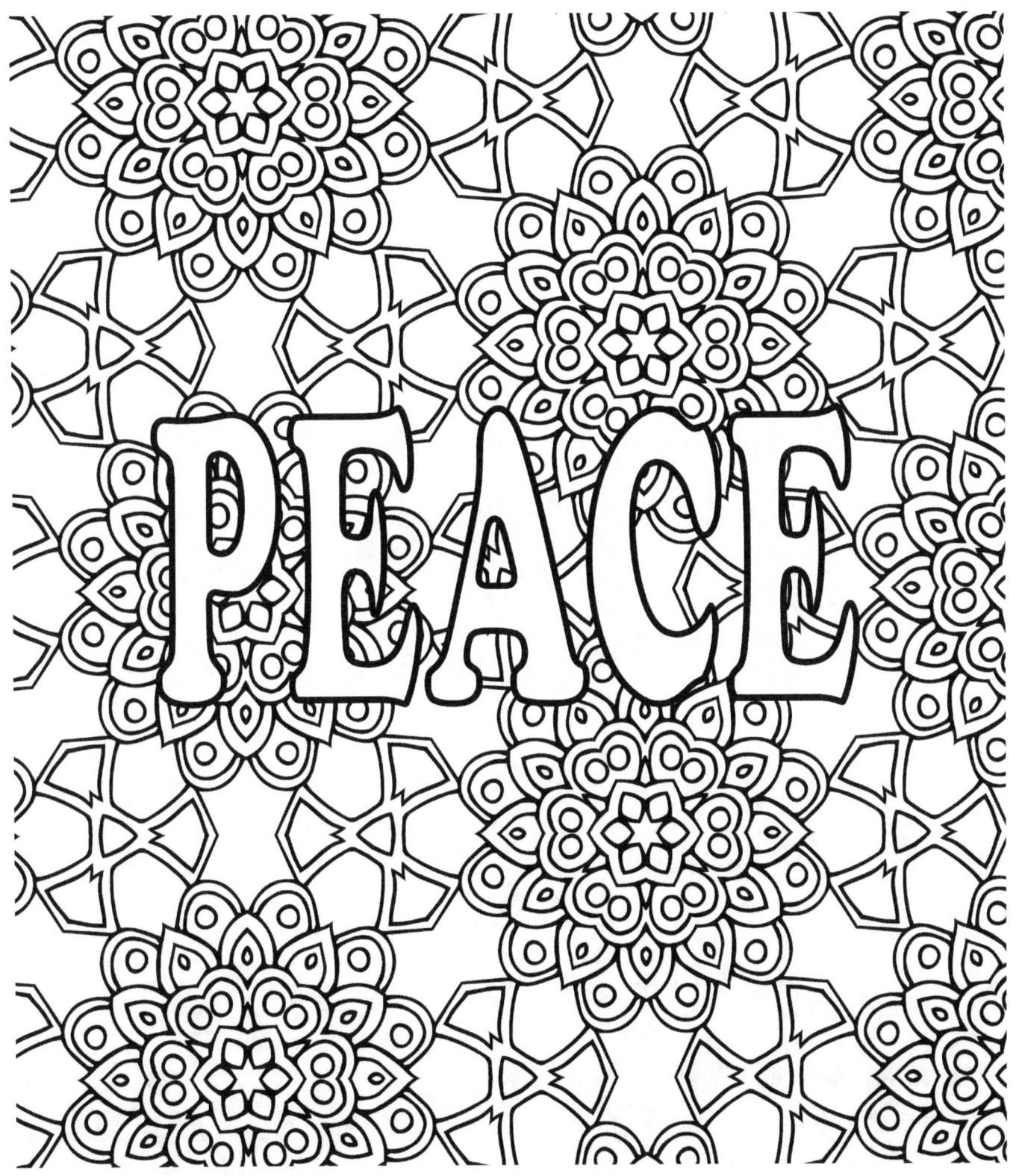

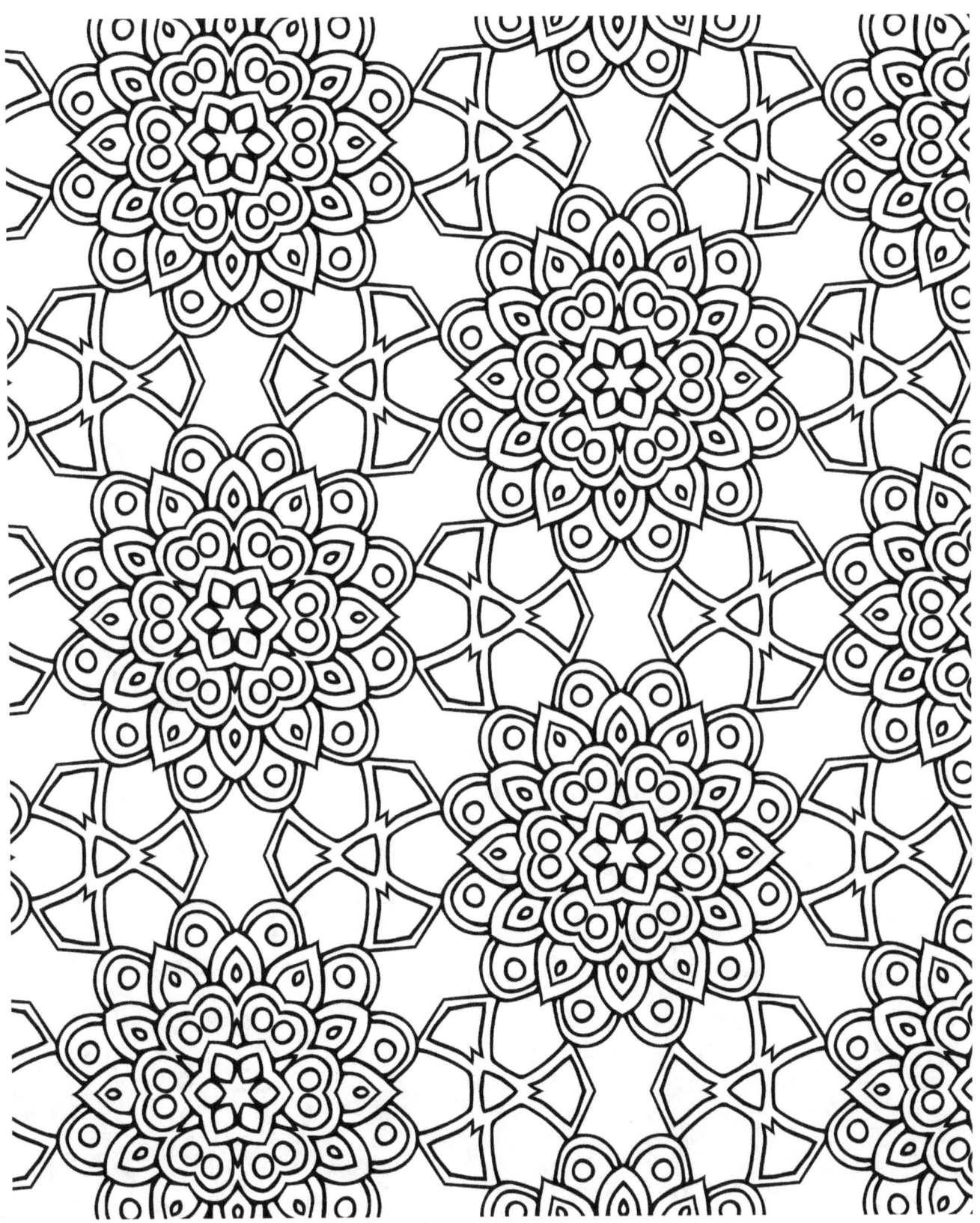

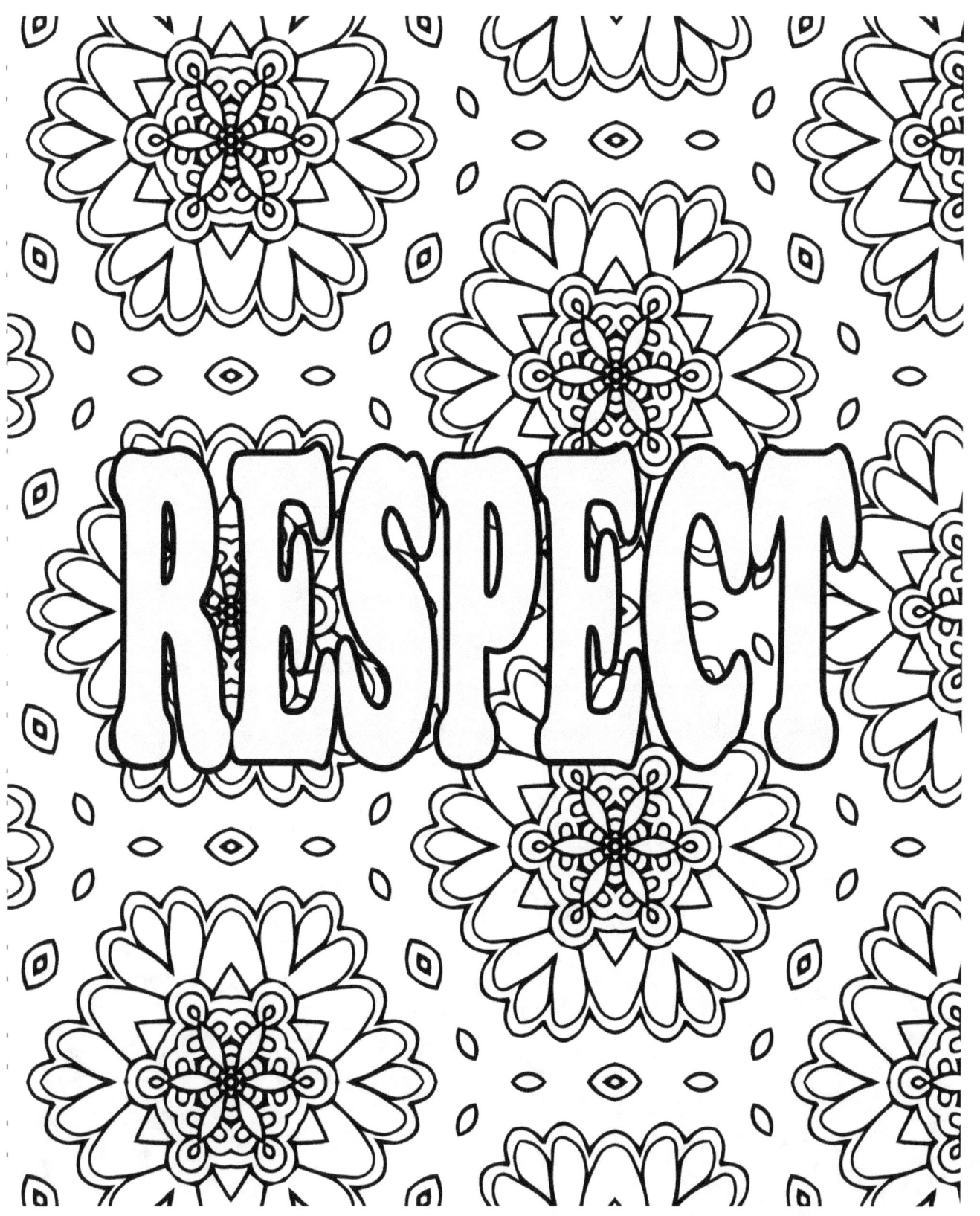

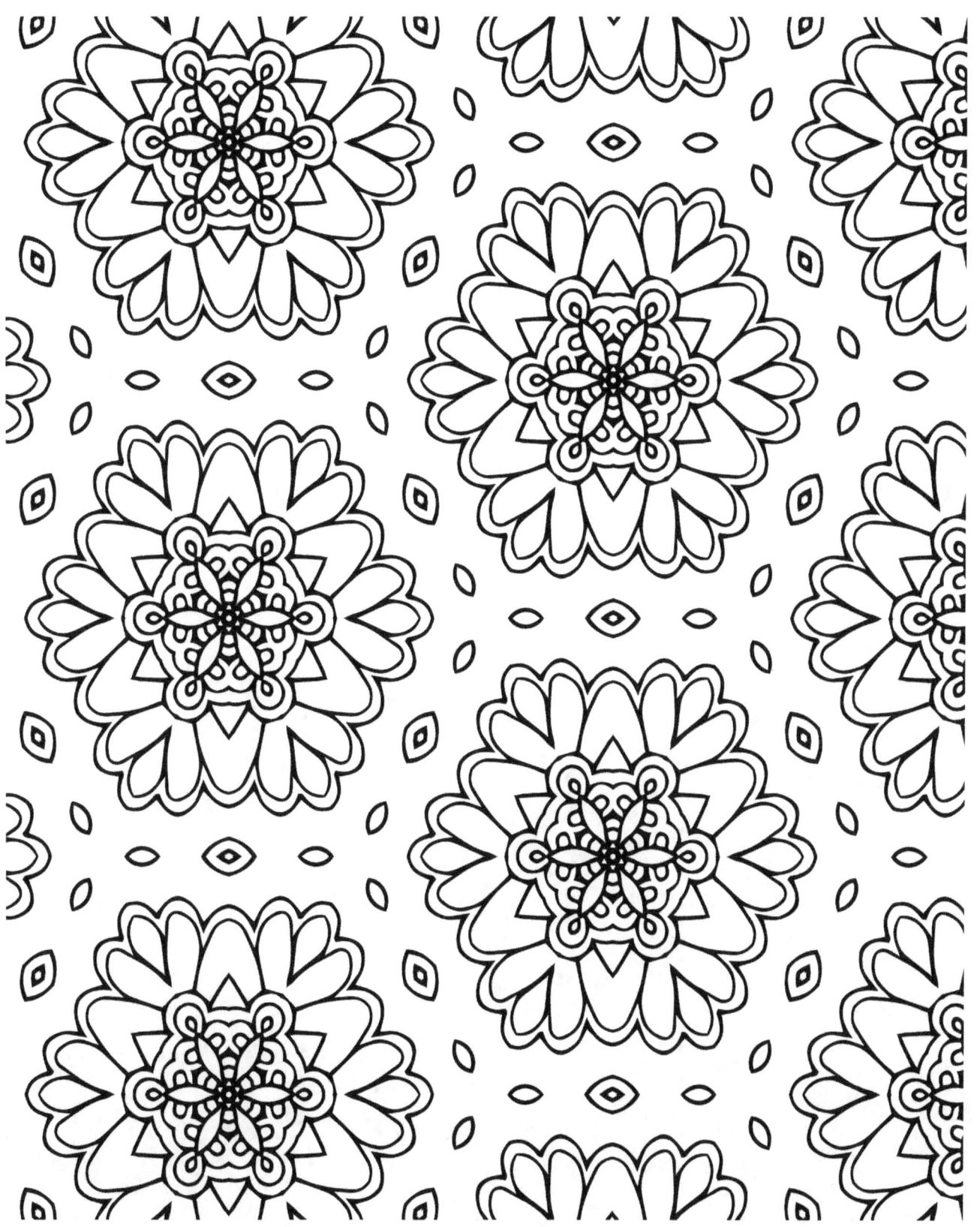

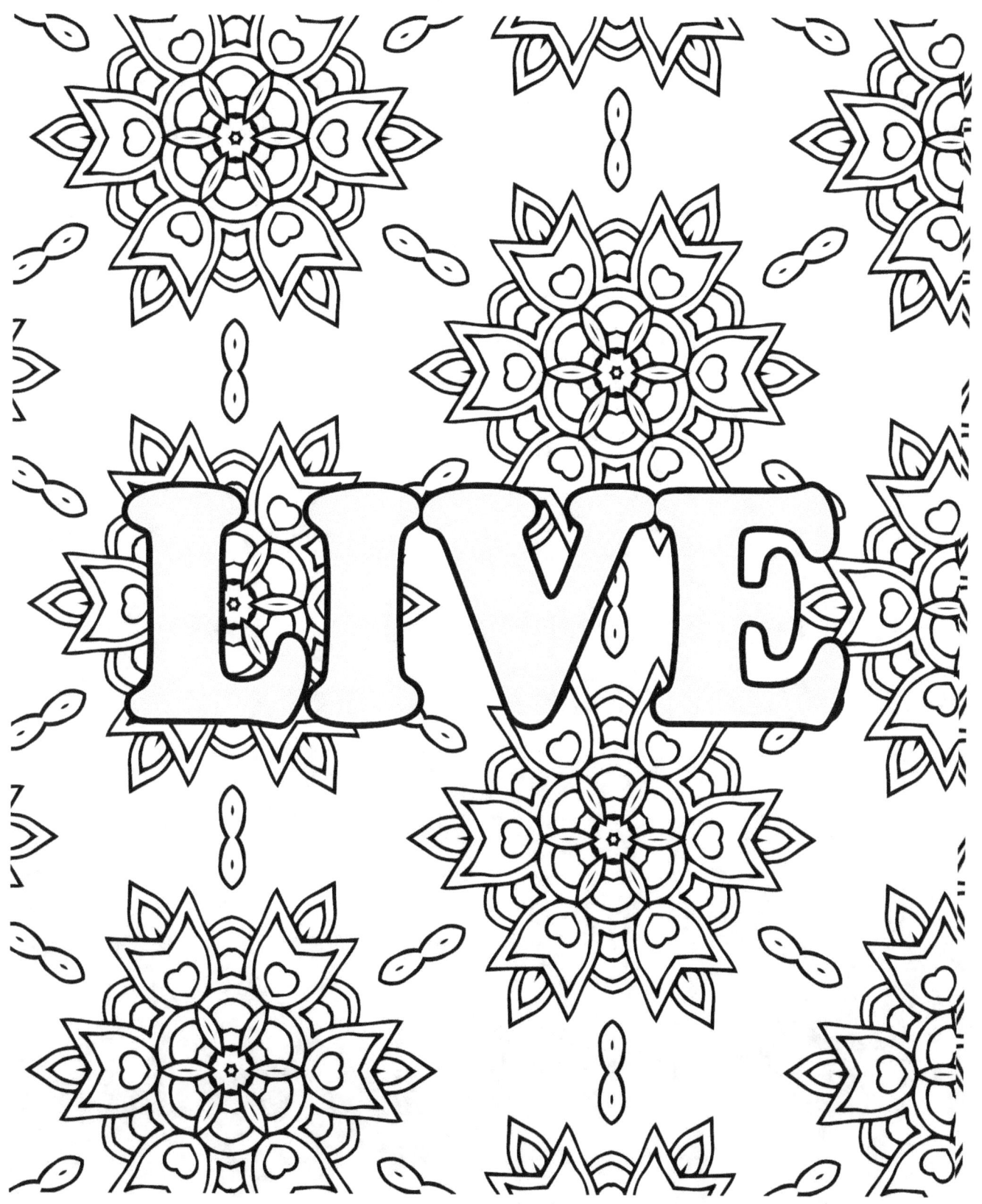

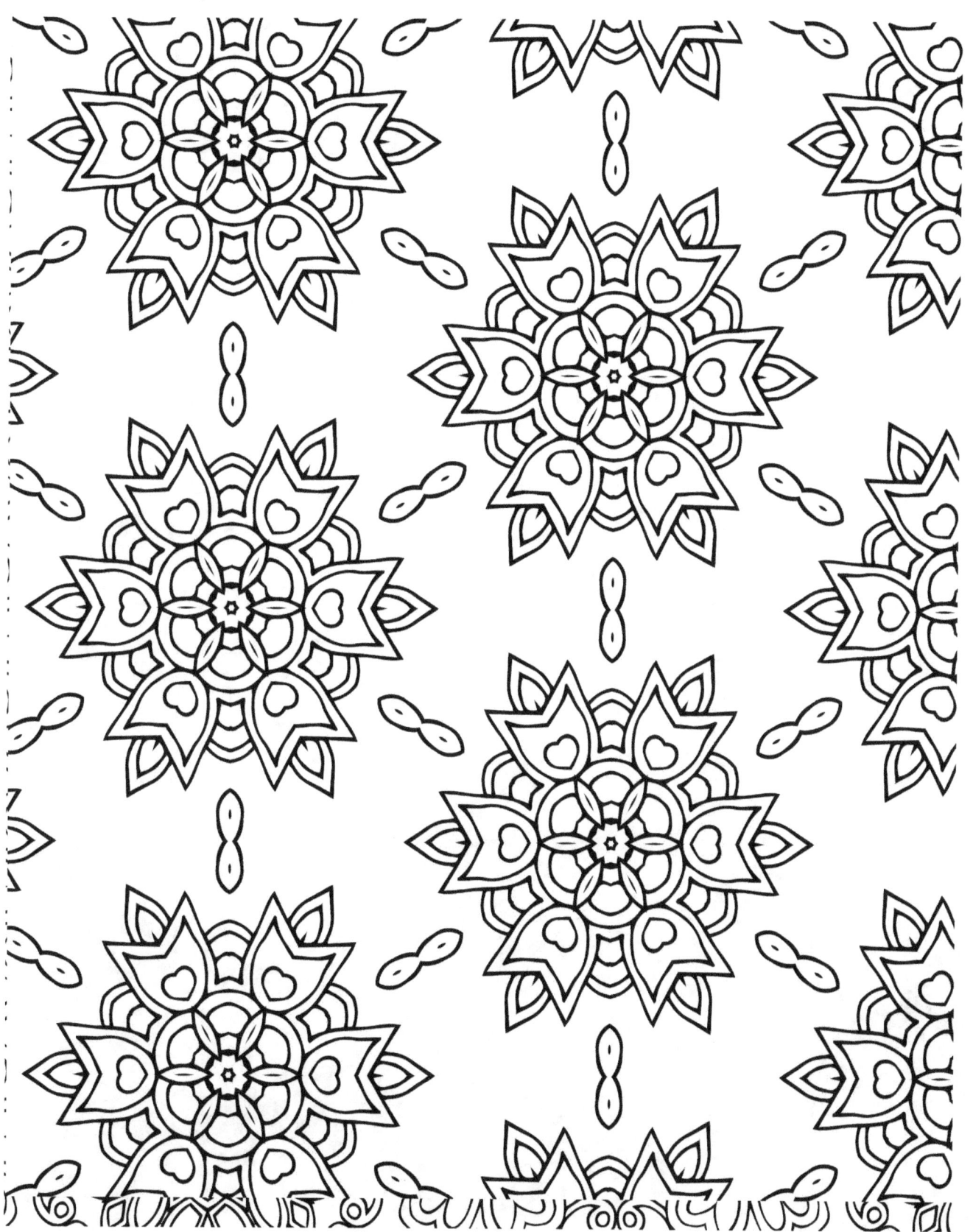

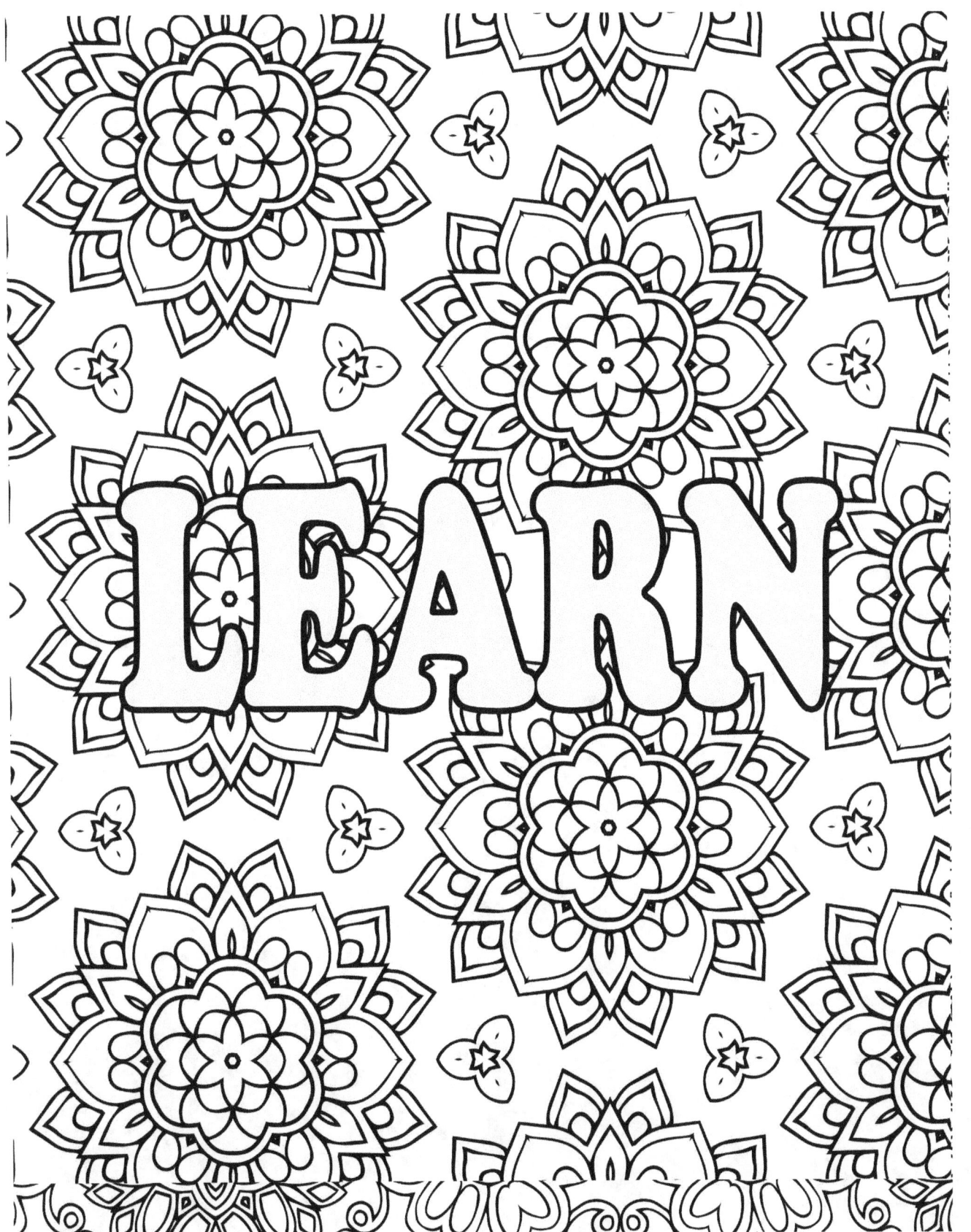

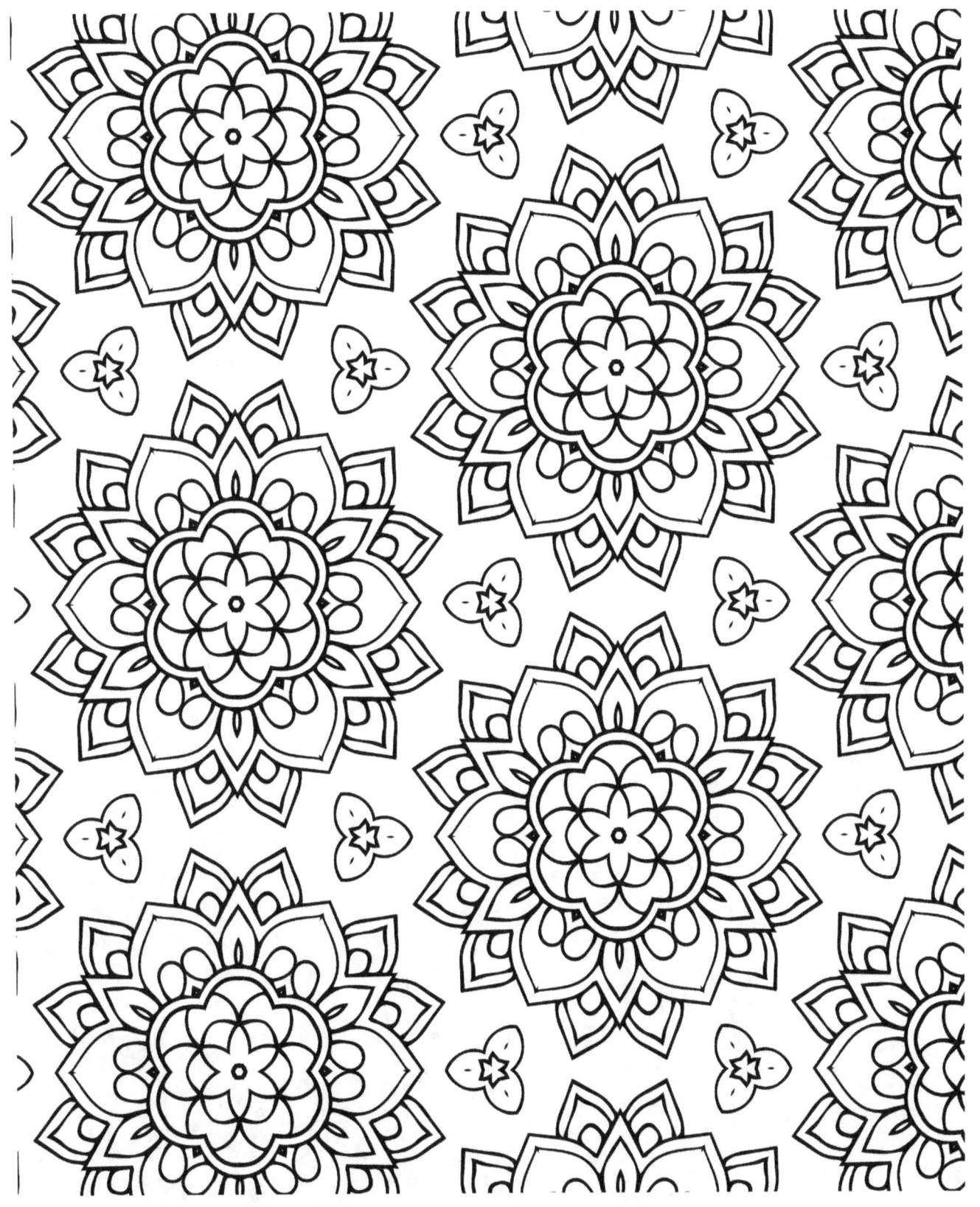

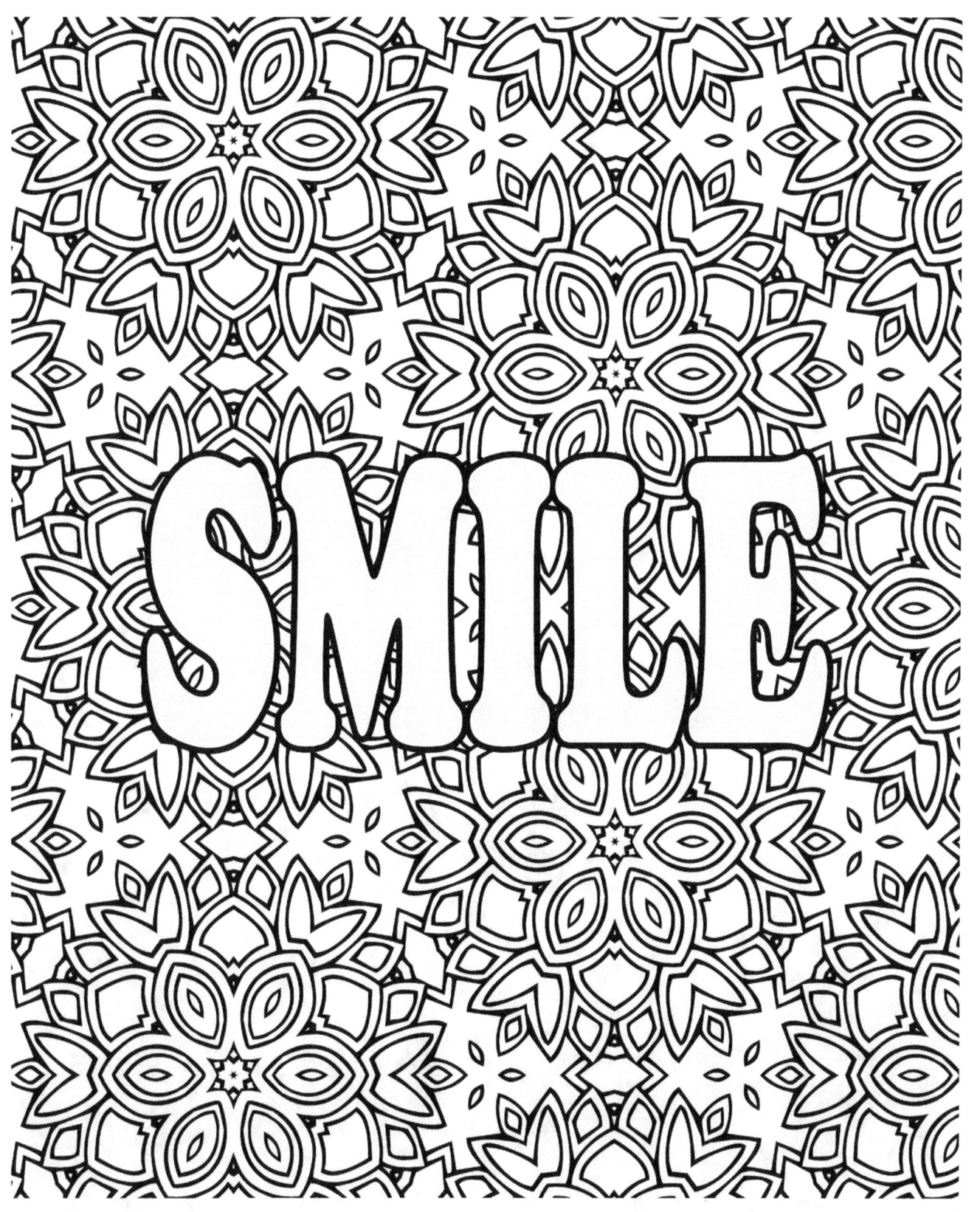

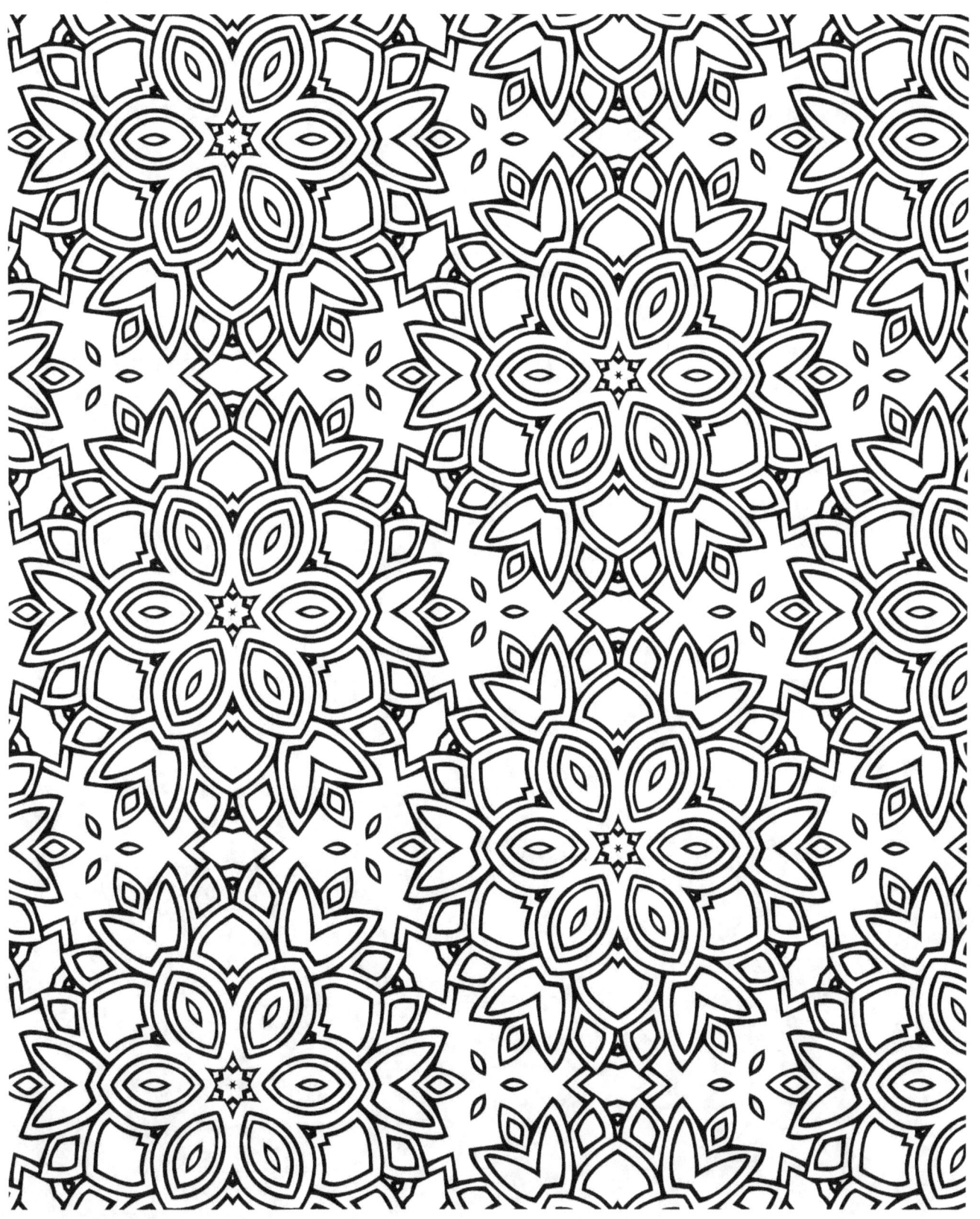

STAY POSITIVE

About Me

I love to create in all forms. There is no better therapy for me than escaping the daily pressures of life than to sprinkle a dash of color into the world.

I hope each of you enjoy this coloring book as much as I enjoyed putting it together.

Thank you.

www.ingramcontent.com/pod-product-compliance
Lightning Source LLC
Chambersburg PA
CBHW080820170526
45158CB00009B/2483